The Bhagavad Gītā

American University Studies

Series VII
Theology and Religion
Vol. 39

PETER LANG
New York • San Francisco • Bern • Baltimore
Frankfurt am Main • Berlin • Wien • Paris

David White

The Bhagavad Gītā

A New Translation with Commentary

PETER LANG
New York • San Francisco • Bern • Baltimore
Frankfurt am Main • Berlin • Wien • Paris

Library of Congress Cataloging-in-Publication Data

Bhagavadgītā. English.
   The Bhagavad Gītā: a new translation with commentary / David White.
      p.   cm. — (American university studies. Series VII, Theology and religion; v. 39)
   Includes index.
   1. White, David. II. Title. III. Series: American university studies. Series VII, Theology and religion; v. 39.
BL1138.62.E5   1989, 1993   294.5'924—dc19   88-9723
ISBN 0-8204-0527-2   CIP
ISBN 0-8204-2424-2 (PBK)
ISSN 0740-0446

CIP-Titelaufnahme der Deutschen Bibliothek

The **Bhagavad-gītā**: a new transl. with commentary / David White. –
New York; Bern; Frankfurt am Main; Paris; Wien: Lang, 1989, 1993
   (American University Studies: Ser. 7, Theology and religion; Vol. 39)
   Einheitssacht.: Bhagavad-gītā<engl.>
   ISBN 0-8204-0527-2
   ISBN 0-8204-2424-2 (PBK)
NE: White, David [Hrsg.]; EST; American
University Studies / 07

Cover design by George Lallas.

The paper in this book meets the guidelines for permanence and durability of the Committee on Production Guidelines for Book Longevity of the Council on Library Resources.

© Peter Lang Publishing, Inc., New York, 1989, 1993

All rights reserved.
Reprint or reproduction, even partially, in all forms such as microfilm, xerography, microfiche, microcard, offset strictly prohibited.

Printed in the United States of America.

Contents

Introduction 1
1   The Epic Setting 11
2   Introduction to Karma Yoga 21
3   One's Individual Nature and One's Own Duty 45
4   Introduction to the Yoga of Devotion 61
5   Renunciation and Nonattached Action 75
6   Introduction to Meditation-Contemplation 85
7   The Nature of Krishna's Deity 101
8   The Cycles of Existence and Nonexistence 111
9   Manifestations of Krishna's Deity 121
10 Krishna as the Cosmic Source of All Things 133
11 Arjuna's Vision of the Cosmic Krishna 145
12 Unitive Knowledge and Selfless Devotion 163
13 The Phenomenal Individual Self 169
14 The Gunas in Human Experience 181
15 Deity as Both Immanent and Transcendent 191
16 Divine and Demonic Natures 199
17 Actions Correlated with the Gunas 205
18 The Final Teachings and Conclusion 215
Index 241

ERRATA

Page 4, line 19, "*makes*" should read "*make*".

Page 28, Stanza (22), line 1, "*as man*" should read "*as a man*".

Page 58, Stanza (37), line 2, "*for*" should read "*from*".

Page 123, add Stanza (9) as follows:

Nor do these actions bind Me (*Krishna not limited*),
    Who am sitting in
    like one sitting it out,
    without any attachment whatever
    to these actions.

Page 123, line 25, "*economic processes*" should read "*cosmic processes*".

Page 167, Stanza (15), line 2, "*and loathing*" should read "*and from loathing*".

Page 177, Stanza (24), line 5, "*other*" should read "*others*".

Page 186, Stanza (20), line 2, "*which originate with the body*" should read "*from which originates the body*".

Page 207, Stanza (7), line 1, "*good*" to "*food*".

Introduction

Of the many scriptures of the ancient Hindu tradition, the *Bhagavad Gītā* is best known to the Western world. "*Bhagavad Gītā*" (*bhagavadgītā* in the Sanskrit text) is a phrase meaning "song of the Lord." The scripture is a poem of seven hundred stanzas called "*shlokas*" (*ślokah*) in eighteen chapters of varying length. The Gītā, as it is popularly known, constitutes a single short section of the sixth book of the *Mahābhārata*, an epic poem of two hundred thousand lines, telling the story of the great war between the Pāndavas, rightful heirs to the throne of the Bhāratas, and their kinsmen, the usurping Kauravas. The Gītā was probably written at some time about 200 B.C.

In form, the poem is mostly a dialogue between Arjuna, a Pāndava prince, and Krishna (*krsna*), who is both Arjuna's kinsman, friend, and charioteer and the incarnation (avatar) of the deity Vishnu. Of the seven hundred *shlokas* of the poem, five hundred and seventy are spoken by Krishna, who is instructing Arjuna in his duty to fight in the righteous cause that is his. Toward the end of the first chapter of the scripture, Arjuna states his strongly felt (but poorly reasoned) case for refusing to fight against an army which contains many of his own relatives, friends, and teachers, even though they are about to go to battle in an unrighteous cause. In the chapters which follow, Arjuna confines himself mainly to questions and brief comments in response to Krishna's exposition and exhortation. A few *shlokas* consist of narration by Sanjaya, who is reporting the dialogue to Dhritarashtra, the abdicated king of the Bhāratas who is now old and blind. Dhritarashtra is the father of the unrighteous Kauravas.

Chapter One sets the scene in the context of the epic. Sanjaya reports that the two armies are facing one another in the early morning of the day the battle is to begin, and he names, in true epic fashion, the great warriors on both sides who will participate in the battle. But the Gītā is primarily concerned with the dialogue that soon takes place between Krishna and Arjuna, who are standing in Arjuna's chariot between the two armies. Since Krishna is "the blessed Lord," in human form, an avatar of "the Great Lord of the universe" (lokamaheśvara), he begins, in chapter two, his instruction concerning Arjuna's duty in this situation of conflict, thereby providing the reader with the teachings of the scripture. The Gītā is thus a detailed lesson in the necessities of right and effective action, delivered in the specific context of the epic battlefield, with Krishna as the divine teacher.

The *Bhagavad Gītā* is therefore not only a very small part of a long epic poem; it is also scripture. Indeed, the Indian tradition of which it is an important part treats the entire *Mahābhārata* as scripture, though over the centuries since its composition, the *Bhagavad Gītā* has come to be more highly regarded as scripture than the rest of the epic. The word "scripture," of course, simply means "writings," but the term is now applied only to those writings which are considered sacred by the people of the religious tradition to which the writings belong.

The reading of other people's ancient scriptures always involves more than the usual difficulties of translation; and as the Christian experience with the Greek text of the New Testament demonstrates, the difficulties of translation alone are more than sufficiently troublesome. The proper and useful translation of a text such as that represented by the *Bhagavad Gītā* consequently involves not only the conversion of the Sanskrit into English; it also necessitates a "translation" of the cultural context of the work in enough detail to make it possible for us to understand those circumstances of its composition and use which most fundamentally determine its significance to the people for whom it was written. We must also know something of its meaning and significance for the Indian people of our own day.

One result of the complexity of this kind of translation is that there are at least three ways of reading the scriptures of those whose religious tradition differs from our own. We may attempt to get the original meaning of the text in the full context of its composition and use. To do this, however, with the assurance that we have succeeded in the attempt, is really not possible, since we can never be completely certain of the accuracy, in all the relevant details, of our interpretation. We may also try to understand the work as a document fundamental to the religious tradition of which it is a living part. The accuracy of our understanding in this manner is capable of a certain amount of verification, since we can check it against the interpretation of those now living who are within the tradition of the scripture. But even so, we must guard against accepting as definitive the interpretations of one or two scholars only, or of explanations by the members of a single sect of the faith.

Finally, we may do our best to read the text as a work constituting an examination of human experience, a work which may contain universally human and therefore comprehensible insights into the experience which is concerned with man's relation to those other-than-human forces which have most often been treated as being related to the divine or the supernatural. If insights about our common human experiences are actually discoverable in the scriptures of others, it may then be possible to incorporate them into our evaluation of various modes of our own thought and action. It is therefore to the discovery of whatever universally comprehensible and possibly useful insights the *Bhagavad Gītā* may hold for us that this translation is primarily directed, though in order to understand the Gītā even in this relatively simple manner, we shall often find it necessary to examine much that is peculiarly Indian.

I think of this translation of the *Bhagavad Gītā* as primarily a "teaching" translation, in two senses of the term "teaching," for it is meant to present the basic teachings of the Gītā to the Western reader as clearly as possible, and it is meant to be useful in the teaching of the philosophies and religious traditions of India. The translation itself is the product of more than twenty years of work.

Because of the syntactic and grammatical differences between Sanskrit and English, I have added expository modifiers, pronouns, connectives, and such other modifications as seemed necessary to make the meaning of the text clear and idiomatic. Except for chapter one, I have omitted the many epic epithets and the multiple nouns of address between Arjuna and Krishna; Chapter One will give the reader the epic flavor of the work. I have also provided explanatory material following the many passages which for various reasons may not be immediately clear to the Western reader. I have placed these materials after rather than before the passages concerned to let the reader encounter the ideas in his or her own terms of the first reading. The reader will therefore often want to re-read the text itself after having read my exposition.

Many scholars, both Indian and Western, have translated the *Bhagavad Gītā* into European languages in an attempt to makes its contents accessible to non-Indian readers, and several scholars, including Sarvepalli Radhakrishnan and Franklin Edgerton, have provided us with English translations of the Gītā. But none of the translations with which I am familiar has attempted to present the teachings of the text in a form designed to satisfy our peculiarly Western sense of "philosophy" and "religion." I say "peculiarly Western" because there are no words in any Asian language that can be translated literally as "philosophy" or "religion" in the sense of current Western usage, since for the Asian thinker, both philosophy and religion are inseparable elements of the total culture and cannot, therefore, be hypostasized as separate entities.

Probably one reason that no one has attempted a "teaching translation" of the kind presented here is that the scripture is neither very orderly in our sense of the term, nor is it at all systematic. The Indian reader does not, of course, find the form of the text opaque or inconvenient; for to him it has a devotional as well as a didactic function. Most of the contents of the Gītā

Introduction

are intelligible to its Hindu readers and hearers, in spite of what may seem to us its inconsistencies and lack of sustained rational order, because for them both the order and effective rationality of what it has to say are in a very real sense provided by the broader Hindu context of traditional ideas, attitudes, values, and practices with which they are familiar and which make perfectly satisfactory sense to them in their traditionally integrated totality.

I would not maintain that my translation and exposition of the *Bhagavad Gītā* have resulted in a presentation of its teachings such that all of what the Indian reader understands from it is here available to the Western reader. Rather than having attempted to make my exposition of the scripture's ideas inclusive of everything contained and implied in the entire text, I have instead tried to explain the more fundamental teachings of the work in such a way that a significant part of what they have to say is comprehensible to the Western reader.

There is, of course, much in the Gītā which the Western reader may not only find difficult to understand; he may also often believe it to be untrue once he has understood what the Gītā is saying. I am convinced, however, that in spite of the strangeness, to us, of much of what the Gītā has to say, we owe it to ourselves to give serious consideration to those aspects of its philosophy that may possibly be applicable to our own thought and action; for it seems to me that the truth about us human beings, our world, and even our God may be so complex that it can usefully be expressed—or partially expressed—in many different ways.

I am also convinced that the *Bhagavad Gītā* often expresses the Indian understanding of the human situation in ways which can be most helpful to us, and that is why I use the term "wisdom" in referring to the teachings and philosophy of the scripture, though I do not pretend to have explained here all the wisdom that may be available as the result of an even more detailed and comprehensive exposition of the work. The Western reader may indeed find that he simply cannot accept a good deal of what the Gītā teaches, but if he discovers just one fresh expression of a truth already known to him, one illuminating passage capable of clarifying his own experience, then he will not have wasted the time it takes to read these pages.

But whether or not we are able to get from the Gītā any wisdom which is applicable to our own experience as individual human beings, we should benefit from this exploration of the scripture and its teachings in at least three ways. We should get a more accurate understanding of one important source of the traditional religious and philosophical thought of Hindu India, as well as a broader comprehension of many aspects of the cultural context of the Indian people past and present. We should also get a far better understanding than is usual in the Western world of the values of traditional society, since they are in many significant ways so closely related to the teachings of the Gītā as often to be practically identical with them. And even when we are not able to assimilate for our own use the specifically Indian teachings of the Gītā, we will have become acquainted with many intrinsically interesting ideas basic to the thought of a large part of the population of our contemporary world—such ideas as the Gītā's conception of deity, of the nature and purpose of human existence, and of the nature of the phenomenal universe, ideas which must make us aware of the fact that our own Western ways of thinking about the many constitutents of human experience are not the only possible, or even plausible, ways of explaining human existence and the world in which we live.

Before considering some of the philosophical and other insights to be found in a reading of the Gītā, I must first answer a question which may well occur to anyone whose cultural and philosophical roots are thoroughly Western: why should we of the progressive, technologically advanced Western world be concerned to look for wisdom in a book written some two thousand years ago in a land which has known nothing like the scientific and material progress we have known? Surely, we of the Judeo-Christian, rational West do not have to go to ancient Hindu India to find whatever wisdom we may need for the solution of our own problems or for our continued progress.

And of course we do *not* have to go outside our own scriptures and other wisdom literature to discover what we need to know about how we should act in order to preserve and enhance our present civilization. Our own scriptures are certainly capable of providing the insights we need in order to survive and grow in both wisdom and welfare. Yet many of us today feel some urgency concerning the present and the future of our world (both figuratively and literally); some of us even entertain doubts concerning whether our civilizations will survive the many conflicts which now chronically afflict it. But whatever may be the likelihood of peace and continuing progress for our own immediate future, it is true that we ourselves and not the wise men and women of other cultures and civilizations must solve these problems if they are to be solved.

In spite of our own responsibility for the solutions of our problems, however, there is yet good reason, as I have indicated, for seeking whatever wisdom other peoples may have to offer us: their insights may help make our own traditional wisdom more effectively available to us as a result of our being confronted with similar insights in the strange and therefore, to us, fresh expressions of those whose ways of thinking and acting are otherwise alien to us.

Wisdom is always in some manner an integration of human knowledge for human good; and since this is the case, the traditional Indian ordering of their ancient knowledge of human experience may well give us a purchase on our own problems, as well as possibilities for their solution, possibilities which we might not be aware of if we limit our search for wisdom to our own traditional sources, even though our own tradition may offer similar insights in forms now so familiar to us that we are effectively incapable of paying serious attention to them. And at any rate, we cannot lose by the efforts we make to broaden—and perhaps deepen—our thinking about that humanity which is common to us all, even if the efforts take us far beyond the confines of our tradition and culture.

We of the Western world, like the rest of humankind from time immemorial, have long been concerned with certain fundamental questions about our universe and our experience as human beings within that universe. These questions have been asked in many ways and under various historical circumstances of greater and lesser urgency, but they may all be summarized in a half-dozen basic formulations of them. (1) What is our relation as human beings to the universe in which we find ourselves? (2) What is our relation to the other human beings who share our planet with us? (3) What is our relation to that aspect of our experience which we have traditionally recognized as being "of God and the supernatural"? (4) What are we ourselves, that we may attempt to comprehend the meaning of our experience? (5) What are the goods and goals which we may find worth living and dying for? And (6) what is that knowledge which is capable of answering questions such as these, and how do we get that knowledge and order it for our enlightenment and use? The *Bhagavad Gītā* addresses all these questions in some detail.

Like ourselves, the author of the Gītā was concerned with the fundamental questions of human experience, but his specification of them and his approach to them were quite different from ours. It is partly the differences in the asking of the basic questions which make it possible for us to benefit from a body of thought arising in a tradition not our own, since the ancient Indian thinker's understanding of our common human problems may enable us to consider our own formulations of the questions from new points of view, as well as with heretofore unconsidered constituents of the problems thus brought to our attention. Here, then, are the explicit and implicit formulations of the great human questions as they are treated in the *Bhagavad Gītā*.

First, and from the standpoint of the Gītā most fundamental, is the question, *what is reality*? More specifically, what is that ultimate reality which is said to underly and sustain everything else that exists? How is that most fundamental reality related to what is good in human experience? What is its relation to knowledge and truth? What is man's relation to this supreme reality? And how is this reality related to phenomenal realities?

Of almost equal importance for the Gītā is the closely related question, *what is deity*? Or more precisely, what constitutes the nature, powers, and functions of deity? And how does deity act in relation to the world and humankind?

What is the world (universe) *made of*? What is the nature of the phenomenal reality of man's ordinary experience? And what is man's place in this world?

What is man himself? What constitutes his individuality, his phenomenal self and psyche? What is man's purpose in life? What are the goods and goals which he may legitimately and effectively seek? What is human action, and how must man act if he is to attain his highest good? What is knowledge, and how is it related to action and to the attainment of human good? What is faith, and what is proper devotion to deity? What is man's proper relation to his fellow creatures in this world? To these and corollary questions concerning human actions and values, the Gītā devotes much of its explicit teaching, since the poem's setting in the epic demands it—Arjuna wants to know what he should do and why he should do it in the specific situation facing him.

Finally, *what is a truly good human being*? What constitutes human perfection? What is such a person like, and what characterizes the conduct, character, and consciousness of a truly good human being?

I have listed the questions in this order because this is roughly the order in which they are addressed in the Gītā. But their appearance there is by no means systematic or completely consistent with this ordering of them. They are, in fact, addressed and re-addressed throughout the text of the poem. One of the functions of the explanatory material, therefore, is to minimize any difficulties resulting from the unsystematic nature of the scripture by emphasizing two traditional points of view (*darśanāh*, "philosophies") which underlie much of the philosophy of the Gītā, both explicitly and implicitly.

This is not meant to imply that the *Bhagavad Gītā* provides a systematic account of these two bodies of thought; but the scripture does contain an appreciable amount of material which is compatible with the later, more fully articulated philosophies known as Samkhya and Vedanta. I therefore find it helpful to explain much of what the Gītā has to say about the various realities noted above in terms of both the earlier and later development of those two systems of thought. I also believe that that part of the Gītā which is in this restricted sense fundamentally congruent with the Samkhya and Vedanta philosophies is an important and interesting aspect of what the Gītā teaches, important not only to the Indian reader but to all who would have a better understanding of the human condition.

Finally, a note about the typography and format of this translation and exposition. The *shlokas* of the text are numbered in the order of Franklin Edgerton's transliterated Sanskrit text. Many *shlokas* are preceded by topical headings, indicating the subject matter to be discussed. I have occasionally included Sanskrit words and phrases; I have included them in parentheses (as in this introduction) so that those readers who know Sanskrit may see what Sanskrit terms I have translated in a particular manner. I often leave untranslated certain Sanskrit words, terms which will have become familiar to the reader through my earlier exposition of them.

The expository material is headed with the numbers of the *shloka* or *shlokas* to be explained and a topical heading denoting the nature of the material contained in the numbered *shlokas*. Occasionally the reader will notice a wider than usual spacing between the *shlokas* of the translated text, indicating that there is a noticeable change of subject at that point. There are no footnotes because this translation is not directed primarily to the attention of Sanskritists or other Indologists, though those readers who are familiar with the Sanskrit text will note my indebtedness to the many scholars who have contributed to our understanding of the text and teachings of the Gītā.

1

The Epic Setting

The *Bhagavad Gītā* begins when the blind Dhritarashtra, father of the usurping Kauravas, asks Sanjaya to tell him what is happening on the battlefield before the battle begins. (In this chapter I have included all the epic epithets and nouns of address to give the reader a sample of the epic flavor of the Sanskrit text.)

The Mythic and Epic Setting

Dhritarashtra said:

(1) On the Field of Righteousness (*dharmakshetre*),

   on the Field of the Kurus,

drawn up ready for battle are my men

   and the sons of Pāndu—

what did they do, Sanjaya?

   (1) The dual nature of the war. The very first half-line of the Gita makes it plain that what is to follow involves not only the epic battle of the Kauravas and the Pāndavas but the perennial battle of good and evil, righteousness (*dharma*) and unrighteousness (*adharma*), in the world of human action and in the human mind.

Sanjaya said:

(2) Seeing the army of the sons of Pāndu gathered there,
> the royal Duryodhana then went to Drona, the teacher,
>> and spoke these words:

(3) 'Teacher, behold this great army
>> of the sons of Pāndu
> brought together by your able student,
>> the son of Drupada (Yudisthira, the eldest son).

(4) 'Here are great warriors, great bowmen,
>> the equal of Bhīma and Arjuna in battle,
> Yuyudhana and Virāta
>> as well as Drupada of the great chariot;

(5) 'Dhrishtaku, Chekitāna,
>> and the hero-king of Kāshi (Banaras),
> Purujit and Kunītbhoja,
>> and that bull of a man, the Shibis' king;

(6) 'Brave Yudhāman and heroic Uttamanjas,
>> Subhadrā's sons and the sons of Draupadī—
> truly all men of great chariots.

(7) 'But, great Brahmin, hear from me now
>> who are the best of our men,
> the leaders of my armies;
>> I shall tell you by naming them.

The Epic Setting

(8) 'Your honored self, Bhīshma, and Karna,
   as well as Kripa, winner of battles,
Ashvatthāman, Vicharna,
   and also the sons of Somadatta,

(9) 'as well as many more heroes
   armed with various weapons,
all of them skillful in battle
   and ready to give up their lives for my sake.

(10) 'Though hardly enough in numbers,
   this army of ours is under
   the protection of Bhīshma,
and though their army is large enough,
   it is only under the protection of Bhīma.

(11) 'Therefore, wherever you are placed
   and in whatever actions,
every one of you must protect Bhīshma above all.'

(12) Giving joy to his heart,
   the brave old grandfather of the Kurus
roared like a rampant lion
   and then blew his conch-horn.

- (13) Then conches, large and small drums,
    - cymbals, and trumpets,
  - and there was a great sound.
- (14) And then, standing in the great chariot
    - with the harnessed white horses,
  - Madhava (Krishna) and the son of Pāndu (Arjuna)
    - blew their own mighty conches.
- (15) Hrishīkesha (Krishna) blew "Pāunchajanya,"
    - Dhanamjaya (Arjuna) blew "Devadatta,"
  - and the wolf-like Bhīma, he of fierce actions,
    - blew the huge conch "Paundra."
- (16) King Yudishthira, son of Kuntī,
    - blew his "Anantvijaya"; Nakule and Sahadeva
  - sounded "Sughosh" and "Manipushpaka."
- (17) And the great bowman, King of Banaras,
    - Shikhandin of the great chariot,
  - Dhrishtadyumna, Virāta,
    - and Sātyaki the unconquered,
- (18) Drupada and the sons of Draupadī,
    - and Subhadrā's well-armed son,
  - all blew their conches
    - one after the other.

The Epic Setting

(19) The great sound tore at the hearts
> of Dhritarashtra's men, swelling upward,

making both sky and earth reverberate.

(20) Then when the roar of battle began,
> Arjuna, son of Pāndu, with his ape-banner,

seeing Dhritarashtra's men drawn up before him,
> raised his bow on high;

(21) and then, O King,
> he spoke these words to Krishna:

'Stop my chariot
> between the two armies, O unshakeable One,

(22) 'so that I can see those who are drawn up here
> ready for battle,

those whom I must fight
> in this great warring action.

(23) 'I shall observe those who are about to do battle,
> those who are gathered here

eager to fight
> for the evil-minded son of Dhritarashtra.

(24) Addressed in this manner by Arjuna,

Krishna stopped the great chariot
> between the two armies,

(25) right in front of Bhīshma and Drona
and all the rulers;
and then he said: 'Son of Prithā (Arjuna),
behold all these Kurus gathered here!'
(26) There Arjuna saw fathers, grandfathers, teachers,
uncles, brothers, sons, grandsons, and friends,
(27) as well as fathers-in-law and old companions.
Seeing all these
and also his own kinsmen assembled here,
(28) Arjuna was filled with deep compassion,
and, dejected, he spoke these words:
'Seeing my own kinsmen here, Krishna,
those who have come here ready to do battle,
(29) 'my legs grow weak
and my mouth is dry.
My body is trembling
and my hair rises up.
(30) 'My bow Gandiva drops from my hand
and even my skin is burning.
I cannot remain still,
and my mind is wandering.
(31) 'I see evil omens, Krishna,
and I can see no good to come
from killing my kinsmen in battle.

The Epic Setting

(32) 'I desire no victory, Krishna,
> nor even the kingdom, nor pleasure either.

What good is a kingdom, Krishna?
> What good are pleasures in life?

(33) 'We want the kingdom, pleasures, and happiness
> for the sake of those brought
>> together here to fight,

willing to give up their lives and goods:

(34) 'teachers, fathers, sons, and grandfathers,

uncles, fathers-in-law, grandsons, brothers-in-law,
> as well as other kinsmen.

(35) 'I do not want to kill them, even if they kill me,
> not even for the sake of ruling
>> the three worlds—

much less for the sake of ruling the earth!

(36) 'If we killed Dhritarashtra's men,
> what pleasure would we get, Krishna?

Only evil would come upon us
> if we killed those killers.

(37) 'Therefore we should not kill
> Dhritarashtra's warriors,
>> who are our own kinsmen,

For having killed our own kinsmen,
> how could we be happy then?

(38) 'Even if they do not understand the evil
   resulting from destruction of the family
   or the crime of wounding a friend,
 their minds having been destroyed by greed,
(39) 'how can we not be wise enough to turn away
   from this wickedness,
 seeing the evil resulting
   from destruction of the family?
(40) 'For when the family is destroyed,
   the ancient and sacred laws of the family
   are also destroyed;
 when these laws have been destroyed,
   then unrighteousness
   overcomes the entire family;
(41) 'and when unrighteousness prevails,
   the women of the family become contaminated;
 when the women become contaminated,
   confusion of the classes follows.
(42) 'Confusion of the classes leads straight to hell,
   both for those who destroyed the family
   and for the family itself,
 for the ancestors will also fall,
   since the sacred rites of offering food and
   water are not maintained.

(43) 'Because the sins of those who destroy the family
> cause confusion of the classes,

the traditional laws of the classes
> and the ancient laws of the family

are destroyed.

(44) 'Then when the laws of the family are destroyed,
> it surely follows

that human beings shall be living in hell,
> exactly as we have heard.

(45) 'Alas, it was a great evil
> that we had determined to commit,

since from greed for the pleasure of kingship
> we decided to kill our kinsmen.

(46) 'So if Dhritarashtra's men should kill me,
> unarmed and without resistance in the battle,

that would be a much better course
> of action for me.'

(47) So saying in the midst of the battlefield,
> Arjuna sat down on the floor of the chariot

and let his bow and arrows fall,
> his mind overcome with grief.

(41–43) The four classes (*varnāḥ*). The classes referred to by Arjuna are the four hereditary occupational and ritual divisions of ancient Indian society: *Brāhmanas* ("Brahmins"), who are knowers and teachers of scripture and law and who also carry out the priestly duties; *Kshatriyas*, who are warriors, rulers, and administrators; *Vaishyas*, who are farmers and merchants; and *Shūdras*, who are manual laborers and servants. The four classes are not "castes"; the institution of caste, though based on the classes, was a much later development.

2

Introduction to Karma Yoga

Sanjaya said:

(1) Saddened and full of compassion,
> Arjuna spoke these words
his eyes dimmed
> and filled with tears.

The Blessed Lord (Krishna) said:

(2) Arjuna! Why are you dejected like this
> in the face of danger?
This is ignoble, dishonorable—
> nor does it lead to heaven.

(3) You should not give in to this weakness
> It is not right for you.
Give up this sadness of heart
> and arise!

Arjuna said:

(4) How can I fight with bow and arrows

    in battle against Bhīshma and Drona,

both of whom are worthy of reverence?

Arjuna Would Renounce the World

(5) It would be much better for me to renounce the world

    than to kill my honored teachers,

for if I kill my teachers, who seek their own good,

    I would then be eating food covered with blood

    here in this world.

Arjuna's Confusion Concerning What to Do

(6) And we do not know

    which of the two courses of action

    would be better for us,

    whether we ought to conquer our enemies

    or whether they should conquer us.

For if we should kill those

    who are in position here before us,

    we ourselves would not want to live.

(6) Arjuna's problem. Arjuna is completely confused about what he should do, now that the great battle is about to begin, whether he should fight, as is his duty as a warrior-prince, or whether he should submit to the enemy. Furthermore, he includes Krishna in his own confusion, forgetting that Krishna is not only his friend and charioteer but that he is also the great Lord of the universe in human form. But he does admit his confusion, and he soon (7) remembers who Krishna is.

One's Own Individual Nature (svabhāva)

(7) My own nature is overcome by weakness

    as a result of my compassion,

    and my thoughts are confused

    concerning what is right (*dharma*, also "duty").

I pray You to tell me definitely

    which course of action is better;

    I come to You as Your disciple—teach me!

(7) One's own individual nature and one's own duty. The *Bhagavad Gītā* teaches that every human being is unique, possessing his or her own individual nature (*svabhāva*, "own being"). Now recognizing Krishna as the divine Teacher, Arjuna becomes his disciple, petitioning Krishna to teach him what his duty is in the present situation. (The words "I come to You as Your disciple—teach me" constitute a kind of formula traditionally spoken by one who would become the disciple of a chosen guru.)

(8) For I do not see what could rid me of this grief

    which dries up my very senses—

not if I were to attain a wealthy kingship

    without rival on earth

    and not even if I were to rule

    over the deities (*devāh*) in heaven.

Sanjaya said:

(9) Having spoken to Krishna in this way,

   Arjuna said, 'I will not fight' and fell silent.

(10) Krishna, with a hint of a smile,

   then spoke these words to the despondent Arjuna

   On the Field between the two armies.

The Blessed Lord said:

First Lesson: Do Not Mourn, for No One is Ever Destroyed

(11) You are grieving for those

   who should not be mourned—

   and yet you speak words of wisdom to Me!

   Those who are wise do not grieve

   either for the dead or for the living.

(12) For never in any manner was I nonexistent,

   nor you, nor these princes here before us;

   and we will never cease to exist,

   any of us at all, throughout all time.

(11–12) The indestructibility of the individual human being. Krishna's first instruction to Arjuna consists of a simple lesson in the traditional metaphysics of the Gītā as it applies to the supposed "destruction" of those who are about to fight and die in battle—the individual person is indestructible.

The Embodied Supreme Self (*paramātma*) Cannot Be Destroyed

(13) Just as the embodied One (*dehī*)

>in this present body

>comes to childhood, youth, and old age,

just so also is there the coming to another body—

>the wise man is not confused by this.

"Evenness of Mind (*samatva*)" in All Circumstances

(14) Contacts of the senses with matter

>cause heat and cold, pleasure and pain—

You must put up with them,

(15) for the resolute man whom these sensations

>do not cause to falter,

the one to whom pleasure and pain are the same,

>he is fit for deathlessness (*amṛtatva*).

(14–15) **Evenness of mind and "deathlessness."** Here we are introduced to one of the most basic concepts of karma yoga, the discipline of nonattached action: it is that evenness of mind in all circumstances of pleasure and pain, success and failure, which is the effective means of nonattachment in the midst of all actions, even those of warfare. The Gītā has more to say about this fundamental teaching, including definitive passages later in this chapter. Note that the nonattached person is fit not for "immortality" (he already has immortality by virtue of his indestructibility); but for "deathlessness," which means he will be liberated from the round of birth, death, and rebirth (samsāra).

Distinction of the Real and the Unreal

(16) The unreal never becomes real,

    and whatever is real never ceases to exist.

The distinction between these two is clearly seen

    by those who know the truth.

(16) The real and the unreal. The doctrine of the absolute indestructibility of what is real and the distinction between the real and the unreal constitutes the foundation of the Gītā's metaphysics, including the indestructibility of the individual human self noted above.

(17) You must understand that That

    by which this entire universe

    is pervaded cannot be destroyed.

No one can ever cause the destruction

    of that imperishable One!

(18) It is declared

    that these bodies come to an end,

but the imperishable One,

    though embodied, is indestructible

    and without an end—therefore fight!

(19) Whoever thinks that he kills, and whoever thinks
>that he is killed,
neither of these understands,
>for no one kills
and no one is killed.

The Supreme Self Is Ever Unborn and Undying

(20) For he, the supreme Self, is not born,
>nor, having come into phenomenal existence,
>will He ever cease to exist.

Unborn, immutable, eternal,
>this primordial Spirit (*puruṣa*) is not killed
when the body is killed.

(21) Whoever knows this unborn, imperishable One,
how can such a man kill—and whom can he kill?

(17–21) The indestructibility of the supreme, embodied Self (*jīvātma*). The doctrine of the indestructibility of the supreme Self provides the rationale (Mahatma Gandhi would say "rationalization") for the legitimacy of killing in a just cause. But we should remember two things: warfare in ancient India was not the wholesale slaughter of both combatants and civilians that it has become in more recent times; and throughout the Gītā the true yogi is characterized as completely nonviolent.

Rebirth of the Supreme Self

(22) Just as man lays aside old, wornout clothes
    and puts on other newer ones,
so, laying aside its wornout bodies,
    the embodied One goes on to other new bodies.

(23) Swords do not cut the embodied One,
    fire does not burn Him,
water does not wet him,
    wind does not dry Him,

(24) for He is not to be cut,
    He is not to be burned,
    nor is He to be either wetted or dried.
He is unchangeable, omnipresent, firmly grounded,
    immovable, everlasting.

(25) He is declared to be unmanifest,
    inexpressible, immutable.
Knowing Him in this manner,
    you should therefore not grieve at all.

(26) Furthermore, even if you should think of Him
    as being continually born and continually dying,
even then you should not mourn Him.

Birth, Death, and Rebirth are Certain

(27) For just as death is certain for one who is born,
    so birth is certain for one who has died.
Therefore, since such things are unavoidable,
    you should not grieve.

(28) The beginnings of creatures are not revealed;
    midway through their existence,
    they are manifest;
    but their ends are not revealed.
Why grieve about this?

(29) One person may look on Him as wonderful,
    another may speak of Him as wonderful
    and still another may hear of Him as wonderful.
But even hearing of Him, no one at all knows Him.

(30) This embodied One in the body of everyone
    is everlastingly unkillable—
you should therefore not grieve for any creature.

Svadharma: One's Own Individual Duty

(31) Furthermore, considering your own duty,
    you should not tremble,
for there is nothing else better for a warrior
    than a battle for righteousness' sake.

(32) And warriors are happy
>to have such a battle presented to them

as if by chance, like a door open to heaven.

(33) So if you will not fight this righteous battle,

then you will get evil for yourself
>by giving up your own duty,

(34) and people will say dishonorable things about you
>without ceasing—

and dishonor is worse than death
>for one who has been honored.

(35) those men of the great chariots will think of you
>as having left the battle from fear;

and you will be considered as of no importance
>by those who once esteemed you highly.

(36) Those who wish you evil
>will say many words that should not be spoken,
>saying evil things of your ability—

what could be more painful than that?

(37) If you fight and are killed, you will gain heaven;;
>or if you conquer, you will enjoy the earth.

Therefore make a firm resolution
>and go into battle.

Evenness of Mind Again. . . .

(38) So get ready for battle,

> holding pleasure and pain, gain and loss,
>
> victory and defeat to be all the same.

In this way you will get no evil.

(31–37) One's own individual duty (*svadharma*). Throughout these seven *shlokas*, Krishna employs an *ad hominem* argument based on a doctrine which the *Bhagavad Gītā* later treats much more seriously—the doctrine which holds that every individual human being is unique and therefore has his own individual duty to perform. Here, Krishna simply threatens Arjuna with the dire worldly consequences of his refusal to fight in a cause which, as a warrior, he should welcome. But the Gītā soon abandons this superficial argument and turns to much more serious matters.

(39) This wisdom has been taught to you

> according to analytical philosophy (*sāmkhya*);
>
> but now hear it according to yoga philosophy;

and then disciplined by this wisdom

> you will be rid of the bondage of action.

(39) Sāmkhya philosophy and karma yoga. Up to this point, Arjuna has been given an elementary lesson in traditional Indian philosophy, a lesson based on what the Gītā refers to as "*sāmkhya*," which I translate here as "analytical philosophy." Krishna now begins to explain karma yoga, the discipline of nonattached action, in much greater detail than in the earlier references to evenness of mind. Karma yoga is here said to be the means that a human being can employ for the attainment of perfection in the very midst of his everyday activities.

Unfailing Effectiveness of Karma Yoga

(40) Here there is no such thing

> as an unsuccessful beginning,

> nor may any real setback

> ever take place.

Even a little of this *dharma* protects against great

> danger.

(40) Dharma as discipline (*yoga*). I have left "*dharma*" untranslated here because though it is usually translated as either "righteousness" or "duty", here it refers to the discipline of nonattached action—the best means, according to the Gita, for the effective performance of one's own duty (*svadharma*).

"Buddhi": Intellect/Will

(41) Single only is the will (*buddhi*)

> that is truly resolute in this world,

for scattered and without purpose are the wills

> of those without firm resolution.

(41) The buddhi and its functions. Here the Gita first employs a concept which is basic to its conception of the nature of man, for it speaks now of the necessity for disciplining the *buddhi*. In the metaphysical psychology of the *Bhagavad Gītā*, the *buddhi* functions as both intellect and will; I therefore often translate the term "*buddhi*" as "intellect-will" or "discriminating will." But, as in the present instance, the term is often more specific, referring either to the discriminating function of the intellect or to the will-function; and once this two-fold functioning of the *buddhi* is familiar to the reader, it is usually best simply to leave the term untranslated, just as we do with "karma" and "yoga", both of which words are now in the English vocabulary without the italics indicating their Sanskrit origin. Finally, the *buddhi* is that twofold function of the individual human consciousness which, in the words of Sri Aurobindo Ghosh (d. 1950), is the "instrument of its own enlightenment" or *bodhi*, and we shall soon see that the Gītā therefore has much to say about the *buddhi* and its crucial significance for human experience and human enlightenment.

Misuse of the Vedas

(42) That superficial talk

    which the undiscriminating utter,

men who delight in the teachings of the Vedas,

    saying that there is nothing beyond them,

(43) men whose very self is desire, seeking heaven—

    such talk results in rebirth

    as the fruit of action;

such talk is concerned with various acts

    directed at the attainment

    of pleasure and power.

(44) In those desiring pleasure and power,

    those who are bereft of right thinking

    by such talk,

the essential resolution is never established

    in clarity of consciousness (*samādhi*).

Vedas, Gunas, and Dvandvas

(45) The Vedas have the three elemental

constituents (*gunas*) as their domain;

you must be free of the *gunas*, free of the dualities

(*dvandvas*), everlastingly established

in purity of consciousness (*sattva*), self-possessed,

and free of getting and possessing things.

(46) So much good as that of an artificial pond

when there is a flood everywhere,

just so much good is there in all the Vedas

for a truly discriminating Brahmin.

(45–46) The *gunas* are the three elemental constitutents of *prakriti* or primordial Nature, which is the undifferentiated material or "matter" that is the source and substance of all phenomenal existence. The entire universe is composed of the three *gunas* of *prakriti* in their various combinations and dynamic modifications. The *gunas* are known as "*sattva*" or "purity," especially purity or clarity of consciousness; "*rajas*" or "energy" and "activity"; and "*tamas*" or "inertia" and "dullness of consciousness." And according to the Gītā, the *gunas* are often experienced in the form of mutually exclusive or conflicting dualities known as "*dvandvas*." The fundamental importance of the *gunas* in human experience is elaborated and emphasized in chapters thirteen and fourteen, seventeen and eighteen.

Karma Yoga: Concern for the Action Alone

(47) Be concerned for the action alone,
> never for its fruits.

Never let the fruits of action
> be your motive for acting—
> neither, however, should you
> be attached to inaction.

Yoga is Evenness of Mind

(48) Being always disciplined and giving up
> all attachment,

perform action with evenness of mind (*samatva*)
> toward both success and failure;
> for yoga may be defined as evenness of mind.

(49) Action is certainly greatly subject to discipline
> of the intellect-will (*buddhi*);
> therefore seek protection in the *buddhi*.

They are miserable whose motive
> for action is its fruit.

Yoga is Skill in Actions

(50) He whose *buddhi* is disciplined (*yukta*)
> transcends both good and evil actions
> in this world.

Therefore discipline yourself in yoga:
> yoga is skill in actions (*kauśalam karmesu*).

(51) With the *buddhi* disciplined

    and having given up the fruits

    produced by action,

those who are wise are freed

    from the bondage of rebirth,

    attaining thereby a state

    which is free of all evil.

(47–51) Karma yoga: a summary. These five *shlokas* summarize the *Bhagavad Gītā's* teachings concerning the nature and practice of karma yoga, the discipline of nonattached action; from them, we can see that karma yoga is the discipline of action by means of action in the very midst of all actions. Nonattachment is simply lack of concern for personal gain or loss as the result of our actions, and it is experienced as what the Gītā refers to as "evenness of mind toward both success and failure." That this does not mean either *de*tachment or indifference is made clear when the Gītā tells us that we should "be concerned for the action" that we perform—and that that concern will be expressed as "skill in actions." The necessary evenness of mind and skill in actions are made possible by control (discipline) of the *buddhi*, that function of human consciousness which is capable of directing and controlling human actions.

The Disciplined Buddhi

(52) When your *buddhi* had passed through

    the jungle of delusion,

then will you come to aversion

    for what is to be heard in the Vedas.

(53) When your *buddhi*, averse to scripture,

> stands unmoving
>
> and immovable in clarity of consciousness
>
> (*samādhi*),

then will you have attained yoga.

(52–53) Karma yoga as discipline of the buddhi. In *shloka* 39, Krishna told Arjuna that the teaching he was about to hear is "according to yoga," and he then proceeded to explain the nature and function of karma yoga. For the Gītā, the discipline of nonattached action constitutes a yoga because it functions as all yogas do, to still the mind, here specified as that function of human consciousness known as "*buddhi*," and to bring it to that "clarity of consciousness" known in the Yoga philosophy as "*samādhi*," in which state the yogi is capable of perfect control of himself and his actions.

Arjuna said:

The Man of Disciplined Buddhi

(54) What is the character of the man

> of established *buddhi*?

How would a man of established *buddhi* speak?

> How would he sit? How would he act?

The Blessed Lord said:

(55) when he throws off all the selfish desires
> that are in his mind (*manas*, "the sense-mind"),
> finding his satisfaction by means of the self
> in the Self alone,

then is he truly declared to be of established
> *buddhi*.

(56) When his mind is not disturbed by sorrows
> and he has lost all desire for pleasures,

when his passion, fear, and anger are all gone,
> he is then truly declared
> to be a man of established *buddhi*.

Evenness of Mind

(57) He who has no desire for any thing,
> who, getting this or that good or ill,
> is neither overjoyed by the one
> nor rejects the other,

his *buddhi* is fully established.

Restraint of the Senses

(58) And when like a turtle withdrawing
> his legs on all sides,
> he withdraws the senses
> from the objects of sensation,

then is his wisdom (*prajna*) fully established.

(59) Except for taste, the objects

> of the senses turn away
>
> from one who is abstemious with food,

but even taste turns away from him

> who has experienced the Supreme (*param*).

(54–59) The senses, the sense-mind, the buddhi and the supreme Self. Arjuna is not a practiced yogi, and he is anything but a philosopher; he therefore asks Krishna a simple, practical question: how is the man of established *buddhi* to be recognized? Krishna answers by saying that such a man controls and restrains his senses by means of his *manas*, a function of human consciousness which I often refer to as the "sense-mind" because for the yogi it is the *manas*, sometimes known as the "eleventh sense," that is capable of controlling the senses. But Krishna also insists that such a man not only restrains the senses; he completely eliminates the selfish desires that arise as a result of the operation of the senses, finding all "his satisfaction by means of the self in the (supreme) Self alone." It is this turning of the *buddhi* to the supreme Self which constitutes its "establishment," its experiencing of that supreme Reality rather than the things and desires of the senses. But of course such control of the senses, the *manas*, and the *buddhi* is not easy to achieve and maintain.

The Senses Are Hard to Control

(60) But the disturbing senses

> may violently carry away the *manas*
>
> even of the man of discrimination

who works hard at this discipline.

Krishna Identified as the Highest Goal

(61) So restraining all the senses,

> one should sit disciplined,
>
> with Me (Krishna) as his highest goal;

for anyone whose senses

> are controlled in this manner,
>
> his wisdom is fully established.

(61) Krishna as supreme deity the highest goal of the practice of yoga. Here we are introduced to one of the central themes of the *Bhagavad Gītā*: Krishna, the "great Lord of the universe," is Himself the highest goal of the yogi, which means that the discipline of nonattached action, karma yoga, may be consummated in a further discipline known as "*bhakti yoga*," the discipline of selfless devotion to deity. The nature of this discipline and its relation to karma yoga are explained in detail in later chapters of the text.

Attachment to Objects of the Senses

(62) Whenever a man gives his attention

> to the objects of the senses,
>
> attachment to those objects arises,

and from attachment springs desire,

> from desire comes anger,

(63) from anger comes great confusion, from confusion

> loss of memory, from loss of memory
>
> loss of mind (*buddhi*),

and from loss of mind a man may perish.

(62–63) Results of attachment to objects of the senses. Krishna warns Arjuna that attachment to objects of the senses leads to loss of control and that if the loss of control is allowed to follow its course, even death may be the result. We should note, however, that in *shloka* 64 to follow, the Gītā counsels *control* of the senses, not suppression of legitimate sense experience.

Proper Use of the Senses

(64)   But with the senses unattached

>   to attraction and aversion,

>   thus acting only on the proper objects

>   of sensation,

a man attains peace.

Peace Results from Restraint of the Senses

(65)   In that peace,

>   all his sufferings begin to fall away,

for the *buddhi* quickly becomes established

>   in one whose consciousness is peaceful.

The Undisciplined Person. . . .

(66) One who is undisciplined is

without effective *buddhi*,

for one who is undisciplined

is without clarity of consciousness;

whoever is without clarity of consciousness

has no peace—

and how can there be happiness

for one without peace?

(67) For the senses are wanderers,

and when the *manas* follows after them,

this takes away one's wisdom,

just as a storm drives a ship

helplessly on the water.

(68) Therefore whoever withdraws his senses on all sides

from the objects of sensation,

his wisdom is established.

(69) What seems like night to all other creatures,

in that the man of control is awake;

and where other creatures are awake,

that is night to the man of wisdom

who fully understands.

Nonattachment to Desires

(70) The ocean is always being filled,

    and yet its stability remains unshaken.

Whomever all desires enter

    as waters enter the ocean,

    he attains peace—

    not he who is attached to desires.

(71) Whoever, giving up all selfish desires,

    goes free from craving,

he is free of egotism and self-interest,

    and he attains true peace.

(70–71) Nonattachment to selfish desires. Nonattachment to the fruits of one's actions means nonattachment to one's selfish desires. It is important to understand, however, that the Gītā does not teach that the man or woman of disciplined *buddhi* is to cease all desiring—that would be either inhuman or superhuman, and the Gītā's teachings are for ordinary human beings like Arjuna. One is therefore simply to allow all desires to arise and disperse naturally, just as the waters enter the ocean and become diffused therein.

(72) That is establishment in *brahman*;

    having attained it,

    one is never again confused.

Being established in this state

    even to the time of death,

    a man attains *brahma-nirvāṇa*.

(72) "Brahman" and "brahma-nirvāṇa." *Brahman* is the transcendent-immanent supreme Reality which is to be realized in the yogi's own conscious experience. The realization of *brahman* is also realization of the supreme Self, which is *brahman* itself immanent in the world and in the consciousness of man. This experience of the supreme Reality is sometimes referred to in the Gītā as *"brahma-nirvāṇa"* and "becoming *brahman*" (*brahmabhūta*, literally *"brahman*-become"). This state is said to constitute the total liberation (*mukti, moksha*) of the individual self and the end of its continuing birth, death, and rebirth—it is attainment of that deathlessness which was referred to earlier.

3

One's Individual Nature and One's Own Duty

Chapter three has two main themes: the continuing exposition of the principles and practices of karma yoga and the characteristics of human nature which make possible the effective practice of the discipline of nonattached action.

Arjuna said:

(1) If you hold the *buddhi* to be of greater importance

than action,

why, then, do you counsel me to violent action?

(2) You seem to cloud my own *buddhi*

with words that are greatly confusing.

So tell me now clearly that one thing

by means of which I may attain the good.

One's Individual Nature and One's Own Duty

Karma Yoga and the Yoga of Knowledge

The Blessed Lord said:

(3) In ancient times a twofold foundation of yoga

> has been proclaimed by Me:

that of the analytical philosophers (*sāmkhyānām*)

> by means of the discipline of knowledge

(*jñāna yoga*)

> and that of the karma yogis

> by means of the discipline of action.

(3) "Yoga," "karma," and "jñāna." Like the word "yoga", "karma" is now in our English dictionaries as an ordinary English word of Sanskrit origin. In the *Bhagavad Gītā*, "karma" usually means "action" or "act," though in chapter eighteen it means "work" in the sense of "vocation." Karma yoga is therefore the discipline of nonattached action for the attainment of the supreme human good that Arjuna has asked about. The *jñāna yoga* of the followers of *sāmkhya* philosophy consists in the disciplining of the *buddhi* (a process sometimes referred to by the Gītā as "*buddhiyoga*") in such a way that the *jñāna yogi* may always discriminate the real from the unreal, as noted in the early *shlokas* of Chapter Two.

The Discipline of Nonattached Action

(4) Man does not attain freedom

> from action by deliberately

>> initiating actions,

and yet neither does he attain to perfection

> by merely renouncing all actions.

Inaction Is Not Possible

(5) For no one can remain even for a moment
> without performing actions,

since the *gunas* born of primordial
> Nature (*prakriti*)
> compel everyone to act whether
> they will to do so or not.

Action, Non-action and Hypocrisy

(6) And even having restrained the organs of action,
> whoever sits self-deluded reflecting
> on the objects of the senses
> with his mind (*manas*),

he is declared to be a hypocrite.

Nonattached Action Is Better than Inaction

(7) But having controlled the senses
> by means of the *manas*,

whoever begins the discipline
> of nonattached action, he excels.

(8) Perform all properly ordained action,
> for action is better than inaction,

and even the maintenance of your body
> is not possible

without action of some kind.

Perform All Actions as Sacrifice

(9) With the exception of actions

for the purpose of sacrifice,

this world is bound by actions.

Free from attachment,

you should perform all actions as sacrifice.

(9) Karma yoga as sacrificial action. The traditional Indian ritual worship consists of various sacrifices known generically as "*yajna*," but here the Gītā interprets the significance of sacrifice as being the nonattached performance of *all* actions. The performance of all actions as sacrifice therefore becomes a fourth essential element of the practice of karma yoga, along with nonattachment, evenness of mind, and skill in actions. But the Gītā proceeds, in the *shlokas* that immediately follow (**10–13**), to put this interpretation of sacrifice into the context of the ancient Vedic tradition of ritual sacrifice. The "Prajāpati" of this passage is the deity whose name means "Lord of the Creatures." (When the Gītā refers to the Vedic *yajna*, I capitalize the English word "Sacrifice.")

Traditional Vedic Sacrifice (*yajna*)

(10) Having produced the creatures

together with the Sacrifice,

Prajāpati, Lord of the Creatures, said long ago:

'With this Sacrifice shall you reproduce—

let this be your "Cow of Good Fortune."

One's Individual Nature and One's Own Duty

(11) 'Nourish the deities with this Sacrifice
    and let the deities nourish you.
Nourishing one another in this manner,
    you shall attain the highest welfare
    (*śreyah param*).

(12) 'For nourished by the Sacrifice,
    the deities will give you your wished-for joys;
but whoever enjoys their gifts
    without giving to them
    is simply a thief.'

(13) Thus good people who eat
    the remains of the Sacrifice
    are freed from all their sins,
but those sinful people who prepare
    the sacrificial food
    for themselves alone eat evil.

The Sacrifice Comes From Action

(14) Creatures come into existence from food;
    food comes into existence
    from the Sacrifice;
the Sacrifice comes into existence from action.

The Source of Action: Brahman(-prakrti)

(15) Know that action originates

from *brahman(-prakṛti),*

and *brahman(-prakṛti)* originates

from the Imperishable (*akshara*).

The all-pervading *brahman(-prakṛti)*

is therefore everlastingly grounded

in the Sacrifice.

(16) Whoever does not help turn the wheel of action

thus set in motion in this world is wicked,

merely delighting in the senses,

and he lives in vain.

(15–16) "**Brahman(-*prakrti*)**" as the source of all action. In this passage, *brahman* is to be identified not with the supreme Reality which is identical with the supreme Self but, instead, with that primordial Nature or *prakriti* which is the source of the *gunas,* whose actions constitute all things and all actions throughout the entire universe. The passage thus gives a traditional explanation of the relation of the original Sacrifice to the existence of this world and its creatures and their actions. Note too that humankind is once again discouraged from seeking to avoid action.

Nonattachment and the Supreme Self

(17) But he who takes delight in the Self alone,
> the man who finds
> his satisfaction in the Self,
> all his gratification in the Self,

for him no action is necessary to perform,

(18) for he has no goal whatever in doing action,
> nor does he have reasons
> for not acting in this life;

neither does he depend at all on any creature
> for his welfare.

Nonattached Action and the Supreme Good

(19) Therefore always perform action
> that should be performed,
> but do so without attachment,

for by performing action without attachment
> man attains the supreme good.

Perfection by Means of Action Alone

(20) Indeed, (the legendary King) Janaka and others
> attained perfection by means of action alone.

Integration of the World

But you should also act with concern
> for the integration of the world
> (*lokasamgraha*).

(20) Nonattached action, perfection, and the integration of the world. In this *shloka*, it is clear that in spite of its overall effort to synthesize the various yogas or disciplines, the *Bhagavad Gītā* admits, with the Indian tradition generally, that any one of the disciplines if practiced to perfection is effective in the attainment of the supreme human good—in this instance the practice of nonattached action. Note also that the karma yogi seeks not only his own good but "the integration of the world" as well, and the injunction to seek the welfare of all creatures is repeated a little later in this same chapter. (25).

Act as an Example for Others

(21) Whatever the best person does,

    other people always do exactly the same;

what he holds as his ideal,

    that everyone will follow.

Krishna Acts as an Example for Mankind

(22) For Me there is nothing whatsoever to be done

    throughout the three worlds—

yet I go on working.

(23) For if I did not go on acting untiringly,

all mankind would follow in My footsteps;

(24) everyone would die if I did not perform action,

    and I would be the cause of great confusion—

I would be causing the death

    of all these creatures.

Act Like Everyone Else but without Attachment

(25) Ignorant people, whenever they act,
    are attached to their action.

The wise man should act exactly as they act,
    but he should be without attachment,
    seeking the integration of the world.

Do Not Preach or Proselytize

(26) He should not cause conflict of *buddhi*
    in ignorant people who are attached to action.

The wise man, acting in a disciplined manner,
    will always allow them to enjoy all actions.

All Actions Are Done by the Gunas Alone

(27) Actions are accomplished
    by the *gunas* of *prakṛti* alone,
but he who is deluded by egotism thinks,
    "I am the doer of actions,"

Do Not Identify with the Ego-self

(28) while he who knows the essential distinction
    between the Self and the *gunas*
    and their activity,
    knowing that the *gunas* act only on themselves,
such a man does not become attached to actions.

Do Not Disturb Those Who Are Attached to Actions

(29) Deluded by the *gunas* of *prakṛti*,

> people become attached to the actions

> of the *gunas*.

The man of perfected knowledge should not

> disturb such dull-witted people

> in their ignorance.

(27–29) The gunas, actions, and attachment. Since everything in the universe is composed of the *gunas* of *prakriti* and their dynamic modifications, literally everything that happens throughout the universe of man and things is actually done by the *gunas* alone. The wise man, according to the Gītā, does not arrogate such actions to himself, knowing that the supreme Self, though immanent in everything that exists, does not act at all but simply experiences the actions of the *gunas*. Most people are attached to their actions, but the wise do not try to convince them of their error (and see **III.25–26** above).

Offer up Your Actions to the Lord

(30) Giving up all your actions to Me,

> with your thoughts on what

pertains to the Self,

> having become free of craving and selfishness,

> fight, throwing off your indisposition.

One's Individual Nature and One's Own Duty 55

(**31**) Those who unceasingly follow this My teaching,

> faithful and uncomplaining,

they also are liberated from actions.

(30–31) How to make all actions a sacrifice. The *Bhagavad Gītā* has earlier (**III.9**) taught that all actions should be performed as a sacrifice; here it tells how this can be done—by offering all actions to the Lord. This teaching constitutes a synthesis of the discipline of nonattached action (*karma yoga*) and the discipline of selfless devotion to deity (*bhakti yoga*). This synthesis of the two disciplines is elaborated throughout the rest of the Gītā.

(**32**) But those who do not follow My teaching,

> complaining about it,

know them to be lost,

> fools deluded by all their false knowledge.

(32) Heavens and hells in the Hindu tradition. To the Western reader, the warning contained in this *shloka* may be reminiscent of the doctrine of eternal damnation; but for the Gītā, as for the Hindu tradition generally, there is no such thing as eternal bliss in some heaven. For the doctrine of the "principle of karma" holds that though the human individual may possibly live so wickedly in a specific lifetime that he will find himself in a hell after death, he must nevertheless be reborn once again when the fruits of his evil life, which are finite, have been exhausted and he has therefore suffered precisely enough for his sins. The extremely good individual may likewise be rewarded in a heaven, but he too will be reborn when he has enjoyed his proper but finite reward in heaven.

Everyone Acts in Accord with His Own Individual Nature

(33) A man always acts in conformity

with his own individual nature,

even the wise man—

all creatures follow their nature.

What, therefore, can coercion (*nigraha*, "holding

down") accomplish?

(33) One's own individual nature and actions. Since the *guṇas* perform all the actions of the phenomenal self, all human actions necessarily conform to the *guṇa*-nature of the individual performing them. It is this conception of the uniqueness of the individual human being which necessitates the doctrine of the importance of one's own duty (*svadharma*), and it is this conception of human nature and action which explains the Gītā's insistence on the ineffectiveness of the extreme austerities practiced by some ascetics—for, as the *shloka* asks, what can such coercion accomplish? (Note that this conception of human nature and action seems to anticipate Sigmund Freud's emphasis on the importance of conscious suppression and unconscious repression.)

The Basic Duality: Desire-and-aversion

(34) The desire and aversion (*rāgadveṣa*)

of each sense

are fixed on the objects of each sense;

a man must not come under the control of this pair,

for they are his two enemies.

(34) Dualities in human experience and their effects. As we have seen (**II.45**), one must be free from bondage to the dualities of human experience, those "pairs of opposites" known to the Indian tradition as *"dvandvas."* Here the Gītā specifies the most basic of these dualities—that passionate desire and equally passionate aversion for desirable and undesirable objects and experiences which are the roots of attachment and its consequent bondage to actions. This is the bondage which results in the continuing rebirth of the individual self.

Svadharma: One's Own Duty

(35) One's own duty, even if it is

    imperfectly performed,

    is better than the duty of another well done.

Even death in the course of doing

    one's own duty is better,

    for attempting to do the duty of another

    brings real danger.

(35) One's own individual duty (*svadharma*). In chapter two, the *Bhagavad Gītā* employs the term "*svadharma*" to refer to Arjuna's duty as a member of the princely class, and the term is often used in this way. But the Gītā also, as here, employs the concept to refer to one's more specific duty as a unique individual, basing this use of the concept on the uniqueness of one's own nature, as in *shloka* 33 above.

Arjuna said:

(36) Then what compels this man or that to do evil,

    even against his will as if coerced by force?

Kāmakrodha: Desire and Anger

The Blessed Lord said:

(37) It is desire, it is anger,

> which arise for the all-devouring,
>
> greatly evil *rajas-guna*.

You must understand that this is

> the enemy in this world.

(37) Desire, anger, and rajas-guna. This *shloka* is not to be understood as saying that the *guna* known as "*rajas*," energy or activity, is intrinsically evil. All three of the *gunas* are simply the elemental constituents of phenomenal reality, and they are all three necessary for the existence of anything. The "evil" of *rajas-guna* referred to here is the evil that arises from attachment to actions resulting from desire and anger. The following *shlokas* make this quite clear.

(38) Just as fire is obscured by smoke

> and a mirror by dust,
>
> as the embryo is hidden
>
> by its covering membrane,

so is the universe

> obscured by desire and anger.

One's Individual Nature and One's Own Duty   59

(39)   Even the knowledge of the man
>who knows is obscured
>
>in this way by his undying enemy
>
>in the form of desire,

which is a fire not to be extinguished.

The Sources of All Desires

(40)   The foundation of this desire
>is said to consist of the senses,
>
>the *manas*, and the *buddhi*,

for by means of these it confuses the embodied One,
>obscuring His knowledge.

(41)   First restraining the senses, therefore,
you should strike down this evil one
>that destroys both wisdom (*jnāna*)
>
>and knowledge (*vijnāna*).

Hierarchy of Human Consciousness

(42)   They say that the senses are important
>(*parāni*, "high"),
>
>but higher than the senses is *manas*,
>
>and higher than *manas* is *buddhi*.

But That which is even higher than the *buddhi*,
>is He, the supreme Self.

Be Aware of the Supreme Self

(43) Therefore, being aware of That
 which is higher than the *buddhi*
 and strengthening yourself
 by means of the Self,
Strike down the enemy that takes the form of desire
 so difficult to overcome.

4

Introduction to the Yoga of Devotion

Karma Yoga an Ancient Discipline

(1) The Blessed Lord said:
   I taught this undying yoga to Vivasvant;
   Vivasvant declared it to Manu:
   Manu proclaimed it to Ikśvāku.

(2) Handed down in order in this way,
   the royal sages knew this yoga;
   but over a long period of time,
   this yoga was lost.

(3) Today I have taught you this very same ancient yoga,
   for you are My devotee (*bhakta*) and My friend—
   this indeed is the ultimate secret.

(1–3) An ancient discipline and the "ultimate secret." Two traditional themes appear in these *shlokas*: the claim that the teachings have their origin in ancient times and the claim that the specific instruction being given in the present circumstances constitutes the "ultimate secret," the highest teaching. Both these themes recur throughout the *Bhagavad Gītā* in relation to various teachings.

Arjuna said:

(4) Your birth is later,
    and the birth of Vivasvant was earlier—
how am I to understand this,
    that You taught this yoga
    from the very beginning,
    as You have said?

Krishna's Knowledge of Past Births

The Blessed Lord said:

(5) My past births are many and yours also;
I know all of them,
    but you do not know them.

Krishna as Avatar

(6) Though I Myself, the everlasting Lord
    of Creatures, am forever unborn,
by employing My lower nature (*prakṛti*),
    I come into phenomenal existence
    by means of My own mysterious power (*māyā*).

(6) **"Māyā" as divine power.** Here the Gītā introduces a concept, "*māyā*," which it employs in a manner much different from its usage in the later Vedanta philosophy. *Māyā* for the *Bhagavad Gītā* is the "mysterious power" of the Lord as he employs his "own lower nature," and it is in no sense illusory, much less an illusion.

Krishna Incarnates for the Sake of Righteousness

(7) For whenever there is a marked decline

of righteousness (*dharma*)

and a mounting increase of

unrighteousness (*adharma*),

then I send Myself forth into the world.

(8) In this way I come into existence age after age,

for the protection of the righteous,

for the devastation of those who do evil,

and to establish once again

a firm foundation for righteousness.

(9) Whoever thus knows My divine birth and actions

as they are in truth,

he does not go to rebirth on leaving the body:

he comes to Me.

(10) Free from desire, fear, and anger

filled with Me, resorting to Me,

many have come to My state,

purified by the fire of knowledge (*jnāna*).

(7–10) Incarnation of deity and devotion to deity. In *shlokas* 7 and 8, Krishna makes it plain that he has deliberately incarnated in human form in order to help those who are righteous because of the rise of unrighteousness in the world. He then teaches that those who know him in this manner, who are "filled with (Him) resorting to (Him)," may attain his own divine state of being. At this point, then, the emphasis of the Gītā's teachings shifts from instruction in karma yoga to an insistence on the importance of selfless devotion to deity, and specifically devotion to the Lord Krishna. This emphasis continues as a major theme throughout the remaining chapters of the book, and the teachings concerning the discipline of devotion, *bhakti yoga*, are integrated with further instruction in practice of karma yoga and the disciplines of unitive knowledge, *jnāna yoga*, and of meditation-contemplation, *dhyāna yoga*.

Krishna's Inclusiveness

(11) In whatever way men come to Me,

    in that same manner

    do I reward them,

for Mine is the path that all men follow.

Effectiveness of the Vedic Sacrifice

(12) Desiring success from actions,

    people in this world sacrifice to the deities,

for in the world of man

    the success that is born of such acts

    comes quickly.

Krishna the Originator of the Four Classes

(13) I originated the four-class structure of society

    according to the *gunas*

        and their distinctive actions.

(13) The four classes of society and guna-nature. According to the Indian tradition, the four classes of human society are divinely ordained; and according to the Gītā, the duties and actions of each of the classes conforms to the *guna*-nature of the individuals belonging to each of the classes. (And see **XVIII.42–45.**)

(14) Actions do not contaminate Me;

> I have no craving for the fruits of action.

Whoever understands Me in this manner

> is himself not bound by actions.

Act as the Wise Men of Old Acted

(15) Knowing this, the ancients

> who sought liberation also performed action.

You should therefore simply perform actions

> as they were performed by the ancients
>
> in olden times.

The Nature of Action and Nonaction

(16) What is action (*karma*),

> and what is nonaction (*akarma*)?
>
> Concerning this question,
>
> even the wise are confused.

I shall therefore explain action to you,

> so that understanding it
>
> you may be free from evil.

Action, Wrong Action, and Nonaction

(17) Indeed, one must understand the nature of action,

    the nature of wrong action (*vikarma*),

  and the nature of nonaction,

since the way of action

    is extremely difficult to understand.

Nonaction in Action and Action in Nonaction

(18) Whoever sees nonaction in action

    and action in nonaction,

he is enlightened among men,

    and he truly acts in a disciplined manner.

(16–18) Action, nonaction, and wrong action. "Seeing nonaction in action and action in nonaction" means that the wise man or woman will perceive the nonphenomenal Self, which does not act, as immanent in the activities of the *gunas*, and will likewise perceive all actions as taking place within the one nonphenomenal, transcendent-immanent Reality of *brahman-ātman*. The wrong action of *vikarma* is dualistic action, action springing from the dualities of ordinary experience and selfish desires noted earlier. The implication of this understanding of action and nonaction is that those who are wise will refuse to identify with their own *guna*-nature and its activities.

The Man of True Knowledge

(19) Everyone whose plans are free of purposes
    based on selfish desires,
    whose actions are consumed
    by the fire of knowledge
such a man the wise declare to be
    a man of true learning (*panditam*).

Always Satisfied and Independent

(20) For having given up attachment
    to the fruits of action,
    always satisfied and independent,
he really does nothing whatever
    even though he is always engaged in action.

(21) Freed from desires, his consciousness (*citta*)
    and his very self controlled,
having renounced all possessions
    and performing actions
    by means of the body alone, he does no evil.

Satisfied with What He Happens to Get

(22) Satisfied with whatever he happens to get,
> having gone beyond the dualities,
> free from envy,
> always the same in both success and failure,

such a man is not bound
> even when he acts.

His Actions Dissolve without a Trace

(23) Liberated, free of all attachment,
> his thoughts (*cetanā*) firmly established
> in wisdom,

doing his work as an act of sacrifice,
> all his actions simply
> dissolve without a trace.

Brahman and the Sacrifice

(24) *Brahman* is the offering of the Sacrifice,
> and *brahman* is also what is poured—
> it is poured by *brahman*
> into the fire of *brahman*.

To *brahman* only will he go who is concentrated
> on the act of Sacrifice which is *brahman*.

Introduction to the Yoga of Devotion

Ways of Sacrifice

(25) Some disciplined men offer
- the Sacrifice to the deities only;

others offer up the Sacrifice
- in the fire of *brahman*
- by means of the Sacrifice itself.

(26) Others offer the senses—
- hearing and the rest of them—
- to the fires of self-restraint;

others offer the objects of the senses—
- sound and the rest—
- to the fires of the senses themselves.

(27) Others offer all the actions of the senses
- and all the actions
- of the vital force (*prāna*, "breath")
- to the fire of the discipline of self-control,

which is lighted by knowledge.

(28) Still others are sacrificers of wealth,
- sacrificers of austerities,
- and sacrificers of yoga,

as well as men of restraint and strict vows
- who sacrifice the study of scripture
- by means of knowledge.

(29) Others offer the exhalation of the breath
    to the inhalation of the breath
    and the inhalation to the exhalation,
thus restraining the passage
    of their exhalation and inhalation,
    devoted to the control of the life-force.

(30) Others control their diet
    and sacrifice by means of their vital forces;

These Sacrifices Destroy Sins

all these sacrificers know
    what the Sacrifice is,
    and they have destroyed
    their sins by means of Sacrifice.

(31) Eaters of the deathless remains of the Sacrifice
    go to the everlasting *brahman*.
But even this world is not
    for one who does not sacrifice—
    how, then, the other worlds?

The Sacrifice Is from Action Alone

(32) Thus many kinds of sacrifice
    are carried out before *brahman*,
but know that they all originate from action;
    knowing this you will be liberated.

All Action Culminates in Knowledge

(33) The sacrifice of knowledge is better

    than any material sacrifice,

  for all action without exception

    culminates in knowledge.

(24–33) Vedic Sacrifice and the various ways of sacrificing. This long passage details the practice of various kinds of traditional Sacrifice, from the ritual Sacrifice ordained by the Vedas to the self-sacrifice of the yogi seeking his final liberation from the round of continuing birth, death, and rebirth. The essential point of the Gītā's teachings in this respect is contained in *shloka* 33 when it says that the sacrifice of knowledge which is offered by the truly disciplined man or woman "is better than any material (or ritual) sacrifice," for all action, including the various acts of sacrificing, "culminates in knowledge."

The Essential Knowledge Can Be Learned

(34) Learn this knowledge by becoming a disciple

    and by service to the teacher;

  for knowing the truth,

    those who have this knowledge

    will teach you wisdom.

(35) Knowing this wisdom,

    you will never again come to be deluded,

  and by means of this wisdom

    you will see all creatures without exception

      as in yourself and also as in Me.

This Wisdom Saves Even the Worst Evildoers

(36) Thus even if you have been the worst
of all evildoers,
you will cross over all evil
by means of the raft of knowledge alone.

Knowledge Is the Great Purifier

(37) Just as a lighted fire
reduces wood to ashes,
even so the fire of knowledge
reduces all actions to ashes,

(38) for nowhere in this world is there to be found
a purifier equal to knowledge.
In time, even the man who has been
perfected in yoga
finds this to be true
in his own experience.

(34–38) Purifying and liberating knowledge can be taught. The knowledge and wisdom which liberate the individual from bondage to ignorance and deluded actions can be taught by those who have already attained it; and it can be learned by those willing to discipline themselves in the appropriate manner. To teach this knowledge is the work of the guru, and to learn it is the work of the dedicated, self-disciplined student.

The Necessity of Faith

(39) Putting knowledge foremost

and controlling the senses

the man of faith gets knowledge.

Then having attained wisdom,

he goes to supreme peace without delay.

(40) The man who does not know and who is without faith,

his very self filled with doubt, perishes.

Neither this world nor the next

nor the enjoyment of happiness

is for him whose self is filled with doubt.

Destroy Doubt with Knowledge

(41) No actions bind the man

who has renounced actions in yoga,

who has destroyed doubt by means of knowledge,

and who is self-possessed.

(42) Therefore go to yoga,

destroying by means of the sword of knowledge

this doubt that originates from ignorance

and dwells in the heart. Arise!

5

Renunciation and Nonattached Action

Arjuna said:

(1) You approve the renunciation of actions
   as well as the discipline of action.
   Please tell me clearly
   which one of these is better.

Renunciation of Actions and Karma Yoga

The Blessed Lord said:

(2) Both renunciation (*sannyāsa*) and the yoga of action
   result in the highest good,
   but of these the discipline of action is better,
   not the renunciation of action.

Karma Yoga Is True Renunciation

(3) Whoever is without either desire or aversion,
   he is understood as forever renouncing action
   and its fruits;
   for whoever is free of the dualities
   is easily liberated from the bondage of action.

(2–3) Karma yoga as true renunciation of action. Here the *Bhagavad Gītā* insists that not only is the discipline of nonattached action superior to the renunciation of action but that it is the only true renunciation of action that is possible for the individual human being. Chapter Eighteen reaffirms this equation of renunciation and nonattached action.

Sāmkhya and Yoga Are Not Different

(4) Only fools speak of the ways

    of knowledge (*sāmkhya*) and yoga

      as distinct, not the wise,

for fully employing either of them,

    a man shall win the fruit of both.

(5) The state which is attained by those

    who follow *sāmkhya*, that is also the state attained

      by men of yoga.

Whoever understands that *sāmkhya* and

    yoga are really one,

      he truly understands.

(4–5) The way of knowledge and the way of nonattached action have the same goal. Just as karma yoga is to be identified with true renunciation of action, so also is it here said to result in the attainment to the same supreme good that is attained by means of the discipline of knowledge known to the Gītā as "*sāmkhya.*" In their results, therefore, if not in the specific practices of the two disciplines, karma yoga and the yoga of knowledge according to *sāmkhya* are essentially the same effective discipline.

Renunciation and Nonattached Action

Self-Discipline Necessary and Possible

(6) But renunciation of the fruits of action

    is hard to achieve without discipline;

disciplined in yoga, however,

    the wise man attains to *brahman* in no long time.

(7) Disciplined in yoga, self-controlled,

    his senses conquered and his self purified,

his self the Self of all beings,

    he is not degraded even by action.

Regimen (sādhana) of the Karma Yogi

(8) "I am doing nothing at all"—

    so should the yogi think,

    knowing that this is the truth.

Whenever he sees, hears, touches, smells,

    eats, walks, sleeps, breathes,

(9) speaks, evacuates, grasps, blinks,

    he holds to the thought,

    "The senses are acting on their objects,"

Offering All Actions to Brahman

(10) giving up all his actions to *brahman*.

    Giving up all attachment,

Whoever acts in this way,

    like water on a lotus leaf

    no evil clings to him.

Acting with Complete Nonattachment

(11) With the body, the mind (*manas*),

    the discriminating will (*buddhi*),

    and even with the senses alone,

disciplined men perform action without attachment,

    for the purpose of self-purification.

(8-11) Sādhana of the karma yogi. Karma yoga is the discipline of nonattached action in the midst of everyday activities; it has no special initiation by a guru, no sacred *mantra* (syllables to be repeated in order to still the mind), and it has no specific *sādhana* or regimen of prescribed practices, no esoteric techniques of meditation and contemplation. Here, however, the *Bhagavad Gītā* teaches the karma yogi how to maintain that evenness of mind which is the very essence of all yogas; he is told how to remember always that it is the *gunas* of his own individual phenomenal nature which perform all his actions.

Nonattachment Results in Peace

(12) Giving up the fruits of his action,

    the man of discipline

    attains everlasting peace.

Because of action resulting from desire,

    the undisciplined man is bound,

    attached to the fruit of his actions.

The Disciplined Man Is Truly Happy

(13) The disciplined man is happy,

> sitting in command, having given up all actions
>
> by means of the *manas*,

while the embodied One in the city

> with the nine gates
>
> neither acts at all nor causes action.

Only Man's Guna-nature Acts

(14) The Lord (*prabhu*), the supreme Self,

> does not initiate either doership or action,
>
> nor the connection of actions and their fruits.

Instead it is one's own nature which acts.

(15) The supreme Self gets neither the evil

> nor the good acts of anyone at all.

Knowledge is covered by ignorance,

> and living beings are deluded by
>
> that ignorance.

(14–15) One's own individual nature alone does all one's actions. Here the Gītā once again insists that it is the individual *guna*-nature alone which performs all human actions. Ignorance of this fact, however, hides the knowledge of the supreme Self and prevents the undisciplined, ignorant man or woman from enjoying the happiness and peace experienced by those who have given up their attachment to the fruits of their actions.

Knowledge of the Self Destroys this Ignorance

(16) But if their ignorance is destroyed

    by knowledge of the Self,

then like the sun itself

    their knowledge reveals that supreme Reality.

The Supreme Self the Ultimate Goal

(17) With the *buddhi* and the entire self on That,

    with That as their ultimate goal,

    totally devoted to That,

they go where they shall not return again,

    all their sins obliterated by knowledge.

Seeing the Same Reality in All

(18) Those who are wise see the same Reality

    in a learned and cultured Brahmin,

    a cow, an elephant,

and even in a mere dog

    or an eater of dog meat.

(19) Right here in this life

    have those men conquered their nature

    whose minds are firmly established

    in such equality (*sāmya*),

for since *brahman* is perfect and the same

    in all creatures,

    they are all firmly grounded in *brahman*.

(18–19) Seeing the one supreme Reality in all things. The liberating knowledge of the supreme Self results in the perception of that one supreme Reality in all creatures, regardless of their state or status. It is perception of the one supreme Reality within all things which the Gītā holds to be the indispensable achievement of the perfected individual. The importance of this unitive perception is emphasized several times throughout the rest of the Gītā.

Evenness of Mind

(20) Such a man will not be overjoyed

    at getting what is pleasant,

    and neither will he grieve

    at getting what is unpleasant.

With the *buddhi* completely stabilized

    in this manner,

    undeluded, knowing *brahman*,

    he is firmly established in *brahman*.

Joy Is the Result

(21) His self not attached to external stimuli,

    when he finds his happiness in the Self,

    his self integrated in the yoga of *brahman*,

he then attains unalterable joy.

(22) But the pleasures of sense experience are nothing

    but sources of frustration (*duhkha*),

    since they all have a beginning and an end.

The truly wise man takes

    no great joy in such pleasures.

(22) Pleasures of the senses. According to the Gītā, pleasures of the senses are not necessarily to be avoided; such pleasures are not evil in themselves—they are to be avoided only insofar as they may be distracting from the work at hand and cause attachment to them. Their lack of great value in human experience lies not in their supposed harmfulness but in their impermanence and in the fact that they must therefore be recognized as inevitable sources of frustration.

Self-control the Beginning of True Happiness

(23) Whoever in this very life,

> before being freed from the body,

> can control the impetus

> which springs from desire and anger,

he is integrated,

> he is the truly happy man.

Culminating in Brahma-nirvāna

(24) He who finds his happiness within,

> his joy within,

> and his only illumination within,

that integrated person, having become *brahman*,

> goes to *brahma-nirvāna*.

Renunciation and Nonattached Action

He Delights in the Welfare of All Creatures

(25) *Brahma-nirvāna* is attained by sages
    whose sins are completely destroyed,
    whose doubts are cut off,
    whose very self is controlled,
and who delight
    in the welfare of all creatures.

(26) To those who have thrown off all doubt and anger
    those spiritual persons
    whose minds are under their complete control,
to these knowers of the Self,
    brahma-nirvāna is close at hand.

Introduction to Dhyāna Yoga

(27) Shutting out external stimuli
    and establishing his vision
    in the center of the forehead,
making equal the inhalation and
    exhalation of his breath
    as they pass through his nostrils,

(28) controlling senses, *manas*, and *buddhi*,

    the wise man seeking final liberation,

    having given up desire, fear, and anger,

whoever is always like this is truly liberated.

(27–28) The nature of dhyāna yoga, the discipline of meditation-contemplation. The discipline of meditation-contemplation is known to the Indian tradition as "*dhyāna yoga.*" The *Bhagavad Gītā* recommends it as effective for the attainment of the supreme good along with the other disciplines. Nor are the disciplines of *dhyāna yoga* and karma yoga exclusive of one another, for the Gītā counsels the karma yogi to supplement his own practice of nonattached action with meditation-contemplation. More detailed directions for the practice of *dhyāna yoga* are provided in chapter six. But chapter five concludes with a gentle reminder of the importance of the discipline of selfless devotion to deity.

(29) He goes to peace who knows Me

    as the receiver of all sacrifice

    and acts of austerity,

as the great Lord of the universe,

    and as the Friend of all creatures.

6

Introduction to Meditation-Contemplation

Karma Yoga Is True Renunciation

(1) Whoever performs properly ordained action
> without concern
> for the fruits of the action,

he is both the true renunciate and the true yogi,
> not he who lights no sacrificial fires
> and performs no rites.

(2) What is called "renunciation,"
> know that to be yoga,

for not without giving up selfish motives
> does anyone come to be a man of yoga.

Action and Evenness of Mind the Means

(3) For the wise man who seeks to attain to yoga,
> action is declared to be the means,

just as for the same man
> when he has become fully disciplined,
> equanimity ($samah$) is said to be the means.

Renunciation of All Selfish Motives

(4) For when he is attached neither to objects of sense

nor to actions,

having renounced all selfish motives,

then is he declared to have attained yoga.

Strengthen the Self by Means of the Self

(5) One should improve (*udharet*, "should lift up")

the self by means of the self;

one should not degrade the self.

For the self is the only friend of the self,

just as the self is the only enemy of the self.

(6) The self is the friend of that self

which by itself conquers itself;

but to him who is not self-possessed,

his very self will remain antagonistic

like an enemy.

(5–6) The importance of the phenomenal self. The *Bhagavad Gītā* teaches that the yogi must eliminate all selfish motives for acting, but it does not teach that the yogi should try to suppress or even minimize the self, even the individual ego-self. For it is the phenomenal self which is to be integrated by the practice of yoga; and it is the individual self which is the only instrument of that integration, since the supreme Self does not act at all. What is wanted, therefore, is a healthy ego-self and not a selfish ego-self.

The Supreme Self the Same in All Circumstances

(7) The supreme Self of the self-conquered person

remains always the same

in heat and cold, pleasure and pain,

as well as in both honor and disgrace.

Evenness of Mind

(8) His self satisfied with both wisdom and knowledge,

immovable, his senses fully mastered,

the yogi is declared to be integrated (*yukta*)

when dirt, stones, and gold

are all the same to him.

Evenness of Buddhi

(9) Whoever has this evenness of *buddhi*

toward friend, ally, enemy, the faraway neutral,

the one holding to a middle position

between friendliness and enmity,

the one who is disliked, and his own kinsmen,

indeed, whoever is the same to both good

and evil persons—such a man is superior.

(8–9) The buddi and "evenness of mind." The *Bhagavad Gītā* here makes it plain that the evenness of mind which is the very essence of the practice of yoga depends on an undisturbed and undisturbable *buddhi*—a *buddhi* so well disciplined and integrated that it perfectly reflects the equanimity of the supreme Self itself. It is also clear that such evenness of mind results in an effective nonattachment in the midst of all actions.

One Dhyāna Yoga Regimen (*Sādhana*)

(10) The yogi should always discipline himself,

    dwelling alone in a private place,

restraining his consciousness (*citta*)

    and his entire self,

    remaining free from desires

    and unhindered by any possessions.

(11) Establishing a firm seat for himself

    in a clean place

    that is neither too high nor too low

and covered with a cloth,

    a skin, and some kusha grass,

This Yoga Is for Self-purification

(12) there fixing his mind (*manas*) on a single object,

    controlling the activity of his consciousness

    and his senses

let him practice yoga for self-purification

    while sitting on the seat.

(13) With his body upright

    and holding his head and neck motionless,

    keeping himself completely steady,

gazing at the root of his nose

    and not looking around in any direction,

(14) with peaceful spirit (*ātma*) and rid of all fears,

    remaining chaste, controlling his mind (*manas*),

with all his consciousness on Me alone,

    absorbed in Me,

    let him sit in this disciplined manner.

(15) Then, always disciplining himself

    and with controlled mind,

the yogi rests in Me

    and attains to that peace which

    culminates in *nirvāṇa*.

(10–15) The Practice of dhyāna yoga. In these half-dozen *shlokas*, the Gītā outlines a traditional *dhyāna yoga* practice. Throughout the chapter it returns to such practices from time to time, but the reader should understand that the techniques of meditation-contemplation referred to in this chapter are described in very general terms; anyone wishing to practice such a discipline would have to learn to do so under the specific tutelage of a guru who had himself practiced the discipline to perfection.

Moderation in Diet, Sleep, and Recreation

(16) But the man who eats too much has no discipline,
>nor does he who eats not at all,

and neither does he who sleeps too much
>nor he who remains always awake.

(17) Whoever is disciplined in food and recreation,
>who exercises disciplined effort in his actions,

>who is disciplined in both sleep

>and wakefulness,

his is the yoga that gets rid of suffering.

(16–17) The middle path between indulgence and "cruel austerities." We shall later see that the *Bhagavad Gītā* condemns in no uncertain terms what it refers to as "cruel austerities" (**XVIII.5**). Here it makes it clear that moderation is the key to the proper practice of yoga, even the yoga of meditation-contemplation, which the Indian tradition had tended to treat as a distinctly ascetic practice.

Results of the Practice of Dhyāna Yoga

(18) When the controlled consciousness (*citta*)
>comes to rest

>in the Self alone,

the man free from craving for all desires
>is then declared to be integrated (*yukta*).

The Controlled Consciousness

(19) Just as a lamp in a windless place
   does not flicker,
that same description is recorded of the yogi
   of controlled consciousness
   practicing discipline of the self.

Consciousness Completely Stilled

(20) When the consciousness becomes still,
   calmed by the practice of yoga,
and when contemplating the Self
   by means of the self
   he is satisfied with the Self;

Joy Beyond the Senses Grasped by the Buddhi

(21) when a man knows that transcendent joy
   beyond the senses,
   which is to be grasped by the *buddhi*,
and when he does not depart in the slightest
   from that state,
   abiding firmly therein;

(22) and when having attained it and being
   firmly established in it
   he deems no other goal to be higher than it,

Unshaken Even by Great Suffering

then is he not to be shaken

> by suffering however great.

Yoga Is Freedom from Bondage to Suffering

(23) He should understand

> that this freedom from bondage (*samyoga*)
>
> to suffering

is what is known as "yoga."

(18–23) Results of the perfect practice of yoga. This characterization of the results of the perfect practice of yoga tells us three things of the greatest importance for understanding the teachings of the *Bhagavad Gītā*. It tells us that the final effect of the proper practice of yoga is the attainment of a "transcendent joy beyond the senses which is to be grasped by the *buddhi*," which is that function of human consciousness capable of such transcendent activity. It tells us that this liberation from bondage to suffering constitutes another definition of "yoga." But perhaps most important, it assures us that though the perfected yogi knows a transcendent joy and is free of the normal human bondage to suffering, such a man or woman has by no means become a kind of superhuman being who is no longer capable of suffering—instead, we are told that like all individual human beings even the perfected yogi will experience his share of suffering, but that being established in a joy beyond the senses, he will not "be shaken by (that) suffering however great" it may sometimes become.

Control of the Consciousness

(24) Giving up without exception

all the desires that come from selfish motives,

completely restraining the crowd of sensations

by means of the *manas* alone,

(25) keeping total control by means of the *buddhi*,

let him become still little by little;

keeping the *manas* fixed within the self,

he should not think at all.

(26) He must control within the self alone

anything whatever

which may distract the unsteady,

flighty *manas*,

keeping it reined in.

(27) For when his *manas* is at rest,

his activity (*rajas guna*) stilled,

to that integrated man, having become *brahman*,

comes supreme and flawless joy.

Joy of the Experience of Brahman

(28) So always disciplining himself,

freed from imperfections,

the yogi easily achieves the unending joy

of the experience of *brahmin*.

(24–28) Control of consciousness and the unitive experience of brahman. Note here that the effects of the disciplining of the self include the complete stilling of the consciousness (*citta*, "mind stuff"), so that all the functions of the normal consciousness have ceased and the quiet contemplation of the supreme Self which is identical with *brahman* may take place. But this complete integration of the self is not only a joyous experience—it is also a unitive experience which makes it possible for the integrated individual to perceive the one transcendent-immanent Reality within all things and all living creatures, as the passage which follows makes clear.

Seeing the One Reality in All

(29) Whoever sees the same Reality in all things,

> who sees himself in all creatures
>
> and all creatures as in himself,

he is the man who is truly integrated in yoga.

(30) whoever sees Me in everything

> and sees everything in Me,

I am not lost to him,

> and he is not lost to Me.

(31) whoever reveres Me as grounded in all creatures,

> holding to that oneness,

that yogi abides in Me

> whatever the state in which
>
> he himself may dwell.

The "Golden Rule" of the Gītā

(32) Whoever, whether in pleasure or in pain,
>sees the same Reality in all creatures
>by comparison with himself,
>
>he is understood to be the supreme yogi.

Difficulty of Restraining the Senses

Arjuna said:

(33) Because of man's instability,
>I do not see any solid
>establishment of that yoga
>
>which has been proclaimed by You
>to be evenness of mind (*sāmya*),

(34) for the *manas* is flighty, impetuous,
>strong, and willful.
>
>I think restraining it is extremely difficult,
>like restraining the wind.

Control by Means of Practice and Dispassion

The Blessed Lord Said:

(35) Certainly the *manas* is flighty

and difficult to control,

but it can be controlled by practice

and dispassion (*vairāgya*).

(36) I know that yoga is difficult to attain

for anyone who is not self-controlled,

but it may be attained by one who is self-controlled

if he works with the right means.

(35–36) Practice, dispassion, and self-control. "Practice" (*abhyāsa*) here means the prescribed practice of one's yoga, the disciplining of the self which is appropriate and effective for the control of one's own individual nature. "Dispassion" (*vairāgya*) is that attitude toward one's own experience, one's actions and their fruits, which prevents the yogi from falsely identifying himself with his ego-self and its activities. "Right means" are those methods, techniques, and practices which are effective for the control and direction of the self according to its individual nature.

Fate of the Man Who Abandons His Yoga

Arjuna said:

(37) The man of faith who is not restrained
and whose mind turns away
from his discipline
before he attains perfection in yoga,
to what end does such a person come?

(38) Unstable, having departed from both yoga
and the worldly life,
deluded on the path of *brahman*,
is he not destroyed like a scattered cloud?

(39) Please dispel this my doubt completely,
for no one other than You is to be found
who can dispel this doubt.

No Good Man Ever Comes to an Evil End

The Blessed Lord said:

(40) There is no destruction of such a person,
either in this world or in the next,
for no doer of righteousness
ever comes to an evil end.

Death and Rebirth of Such a Person

(41) Having attained the heaven
    of those who act virtuously
    and dwelling there for innumerable years,
one who has strayed from discipline in this life
    is then reborn into the home
    of pure and respected people;

(42) or he may even come into existence
    in the family of disciplined
    and enlightened people,
though such a birth is much harder
    to attain in this world.

Effects of One's Yoga Not Lost at Death

(43) There he is conjoined with the *buddhi*
    which he had in his previous body,
and so from that point onward
    he works toward perfection,

(44) for by that earlier practice
    he is carried along
    even without his willing it.
Even that man who only wishes to know yoga
    transcends the mere word-*brahman* of scripture.

He Finally Attains His Goal

(45)   But by means of working hard and long,

   his imperfections purified,

the yogi perfected throughout many births

   then goes to the supreme goal.

(46)   The yogi is superior to the man of austerities;

   he is even thought to be better than

   men of knowledge;

   and the yogi is also superior

   to men of ritual performance—

therefore be a yogi!

(47)   Of all yogis, furthermore,

   whoever worships Me with faith,

   his inner self gone to Me,

him I hold to be the most disciplined.

7

The Nature of Krishna's Deity

How to Know Krishna

The Blessed Lord said:

(1) Hear now how you shall without doubt
    know Me completely,
practicing yoga with your mind fixed on Me,
    depending entirely on Me.

How to Get Both Knowledge and Wisdom

(2) I will explain to you completely
    both knowledge (*vijnāna*) and wisdom (*jnāna*),
having known which nothing else remains
    to be known in this world.

Few Seek Perfection

(3) Among thousands of human beings,
    perhaps one strives for perfection.
But even of those who work hard and are perfected,
    perhaps only one knows Me in truth.

(3) The deity of Krishna and his relation to the world. In this chapter, the *Bhagavad Gītā* presents its first account of the deity of Krishna and of his relation as supreme deity to man and the world, a relationship which is of the greatest possible inclusiveness and intimacy. The purpose of this exposition is, from the point of view of the Gītā, to prepare the man or woman seeking perfection for participation in the yoga of selfless devotion to deity, *bhakti yoga*.

Krishna's "Lower Nature"

(4) Earth, water, fire, air, ether (*kham*, "boundless space"),

> *manas*, *buddhi*, and the ego-principle

> (*ahamkāra*, "I-maker")—

My Nature is divisible

> in this eightfold manner.

(5) But this is My lower Nature, and you should know

> My higher Nature also:

Krishna's "Higher Nature"

It is the living substance (*jīvabhūtam*,)

> by means of which this universe is sustained.

The Source of All Things

(6) Know that this is the source (*yoni*, "womb")

> of all creatures.

I am both the coming into existence (*prabhāva*)

> and the passing out of existence (*pralaya*)

> of the entire universe.

(7) Nothing whatever exists

    which is higher than I;

on Me this entire universe is strung

    like jewels on a thread.

(4–7) Krishna's two natures and the phenomenal universe. Here we learn that according to the *Bhagavad Gītā*, the phenomenal universe itself, as well as the human beings who inhabit it, is composed of Krishna's own "lower nature" and is therefore to be understood as in this sense divine. But not only is the world and its creatures composed of the *prakriti* of Krishna, it is Krishna's own "higher nature" which is the source and living substance of all things. It is no wonder, then, that in this view "nothing whatever exists which is higher than" Krishna as Lord of the universe. The intimacy and inclusiveness of this identification of Krishna with the world of men and things is elaborated in greater detail in the *shlokas* which follow, as well as later in chapters nine, ten, and eleven.

Krishna Immanent in All Things

(8) I am the taste in water,

    the light of the sun and the moon,

the sacred syllable '*Om*', the sound

    in boundless space,

    the humanness of man.

(9) I am the pure fragrance of earth

    and the brightness of fire;

I am the life in all creatures

    and the austerity of those

    who practice austerities.

(10) Know that I am the everlasting seed

    of all creatures;

I am the *buddhi* of those who are wise

    and the brilliance of those who are brilliant.

(11) I am also the power of those powerful men

    who are free of desire and passion.

I am that desire in creatures

    which is not opposed to righteousness.

(12) From Me alone are those natures which are

    of *sattva-guna*

    and even those which are of *rajas*

    as well as those which are of *tamas*

But I am not only in them—

    they are in Me.

Krishna Not Recognized

(13) Deluded by these natures

    composed of the three *gunas*,

    this whole world fails to recognize Me,

Who am higher than they and imperishable.

Krishna's Māyā

(14) For this is my divine mystery,

which is made up of the three *gunas*,

extremely difficult to transcend.

But those who resort to Me alone

can transcend this mystery.

(15) Deluded doers of evil, the lowest of humankind,

do not resort to Me;

deprived of knowledge by *māyā*,

they cling to their own demonic natures.

(13–15) Failure to recognize Krishna's immanence. Creatures here in this world do not recognize the Lord Krishna as being within themselves and the things around them, because they are deluded by false identifcation with their own phenomenal natures. According to the Gītā, however, even this delusion is the result of Krishna's own "mystery" or *māyā*, his transcendent power, because even the *guna*-nature of each creature is itself composed of Krishna's own lower Nature or *prakriti*. (The Gītā has more to say about the "demonic natures" of those who habitually do evil, in Chapter Sixteen.)

Kinds of People Who Resort to Krishna

(16) There are four kinds of virtuous people

who worship Me:

those who suffer, those who seek knowledge,

those who seek their own good,

and those who possess knowledge.

(17) The best of these are those who possess knowledge,
> for they are always disciplined
>
> and of single devotion.
>
> For I am extremely dear to one possessing knowledge,
>
> and such a man is dear to Me.

(18) These people are all worthy,
> but I hold that the man of knowledge
>
> is My very self;
>
> for he, self-disciplined, has come to Me only,
>
> the ultimate goal.

Krishna is "All"!

(19) At the end of numerous births,
> the man of knowledge resorts to Me only,
>
> saying, "Krishna-Vāsudeva is all"—
>
> but such a great spirit (*mahātma*)
>
> is hard to find.

(16–19) Krishna and the men and women of knowledge. Krishna is here said to prefer the man or woman of knowledge to all other virtuous people, because they know who he really is—and, in the view of the *Bhagavad Gītā*, he is "all" (*sarvam*). But Krishna complains that such a knowing person is all too hard to find. For the traditional devotee of the Lord Krishna, this identification of their Lord as "all" constitutes the *theological* climax of the Gītā, a climax which is elaborated in rich detail in chapters nine, ten, and eleven. (The *dramatic* climax of the poem is contained in chapter eleven.)

Various Practices according to Individual Natures

(20) Bereft of knowledge by various desires,

    people resort to other deities

and take up one or another practice

    as directed by their own natures.

Krishna Ordains the Worship of All the Deities

(21) Whatever may be the form of deity

    that any devotee desires to worship with faith,

for any such devotee I Myself ordain the existence

    of that very form.

(22) Disciplined by that faith,

    he seeks to worship that form,

and he thereby gets his desires,

    for I Myself decree them.

Such Worship Has Finite Results

(23) But those people have little knowledge,

    for the result of that worship comes to an end.

The worshippers of the deities go to the deities,

    just as My devotees come to Me.

(20–23) **Ways of worship according to individual natures.** These four *shlokas* seem to insist on the superiority of devotion to Krishna, but they also contain one doctrine which is of importance for an understanding of the teachings of the *Bhagavad Gītā* regardless of which deity (or none at all) one may be devoted to with faith. For if we ignore the Krishna-theism of these *shlokas*, we find the

Gītā saying that "people . . . take up one or another practice as directed by their natures," which means that the Gītā recognizes that according to its own metaphysical psychology, the discipline an individual chooses as his own means to integration and enlightenment depends on his own individual nature, his own unique individuality. It should also be noted, however, that though the Gītā insists on the superiority of an ultimate devotion to Krishna, it holds that the worship of other deities is ordained by that same Lord Krishna.

Krishna's True Nature Not Known to All

(24) Unenlightened people think of Me

    as having come into existence,

Not knowing My higher, unmanifest Being,

    which is supreme and imperishable.

(25) Hidden by My skillful mystery (*yoga māyā*),

    I am not revealed to everyone;

this world is deluded

    and does not recognize Me

    as unborn and undying.

(26) I know the creatures that are past,

    those that are present,

    and those that are yet to be,

but no one knows Me!

Delusion of the Dualities

(27)   The delusion of the dualities

   arises from desire and aversion,

and because of that delusion

   all creatures are from birth subject

   to great confusion.

(28)   But those men of righteous action

   whose sins have come to an end,

   liberated from the delusion of the dualities,

they worship Me with firm resolution.

(24–28) The delusion of the dualities. Again the Gītā tells us that "the delusion of the dualities" comes from that most basic duality of all, "desire-and-aversion" (*rāgadveṣa*). Here, however, its emphasis is on the doctrine which holds that worship of Krishna will be the result of liberation from the delusion of the dualities.

Knowledge of Brahman

(29)   Those who work for liberation from old age and death,

   taking refuge in Me,

they know that *brahman* completely,

   as it relates to the self and all action,

(30)   as it relates to creatures and to divinity—

   and they know Me in relation to the Sacrifice.

Whoever knows Me in this manner

   even at the time of death

   shall know Me with integrated consciousness.

(29–30) Devotion to Krishna and knowledge of brahman. Thus the chapter which introduces Krishna as the great Lord of the universe, as the "all" which must be known if liberation is to be attained by means of selfless devotion to deity, concludes by telling us that those who "take refuge in Krishna" will know *brahman* and its relation to the individual self and to the rest of the phenomenal universe, as well as the relation of Krishna as Lord to the Sacrifice, which we have earlier been told is the very substance of what maintains man's relation to deity. Chapter Eight then proceeds to explain these relationships in summary form.

8

The Cycles of Existence and Nonexistence

Arjuna said:

(1) What is that *brahman*,

    what is it that relates to the Self?

What is action,

    and what is said to relate to divinity?

(2) What is it that relates to the Sacrifice,

    and how is it done here in the body?

And how are You to be known by self-integrated people

    at the time of death?

Brahman the Self, Action, Divinity, and the Sacrifice

The Blessed Lord said:

(3) *Brahman* is the supreme, imperishable One;
>one's own nature
>>is that which is said to relate to the Self.

That which causes the coming
>into existence of creatures
>>is that creative force (*visarga*, "out-pouring")

>known as action (*karma*).

(4) that which relates to creatures
>is the mutable state of existence,
>and it is Spirit (*purusa*)
>which relates to divinity.

I Myself am That which relates to the Sacrifice
>here in the body.

Thinking of Krishna at the Time of Death

(5) And whoever dies thinking of Me,
>he comes to My state on leaving the body—
>>of this there is no doubt.

The Cycles of Existence and Nonexistence 113

(6) For whatever state of existence

    a man is thinking about

    when he leaves the body at the end of his life,

he always goes exactly to

    just that state of existence,

    becoming that very state of being.

(5–6) Thoughts at the time of death. Here, after summarizing the relationships noted at the end of chapter seven, the Gītā presents a traditional Indian view of the importance of one's thoughts at the time of death—a view which is dependent on the doctrine of rebirth which was introduced in Chapter Two. Whether this teaching is meant quite literally as a part of the philosophy of the *Bhagavad Gītā* or not, it is certainly meant to comfort Arjuna in the situation he finds himself in before the battle, as the next *shloka* makes quite clear.

(7) Therefore remember Me at all times

    and fight!

With your *manas* and your *buddhi* fixed firmly on Me,

    you will most certainly come to Me.

The Yogi Goes to the Supreme Spirit

(8) Whoever is disciplined

    in the practice of yoga,

    his thoughts not wandering to anything else,

he goes to the supreme divine Spirit

    (*paramam puruṣam divyam*)

    to which he has given his attention.

Supreme Self as Seer, Ruler, and Supporter

(9) The primordial Seer, the Ruler,
    tinier than the atom,
    the Supporter of everything,
in form unthinkable, sun-colored, beyond all darkness—
    whoever would mediate on Him

(10) with unfaltering mind at the time of death,
    disciplined by devotion and by the power of yoga,
    causing the vital forces to gather
    at the center of the forehead,
he goes to that supreme, divine Spirit.

Entering the Imperishable at the Time of Death

(11) What knowers of the Veda
    call "the Imperishable" (*akṣaram*),
    which men of austerity
    without passion enter into,
that divine Word which men seek
    by living a life of chastity,
    I shall now proclaim to you briefly.

(12) Restraining all the openings of the body
    and concentrating the *manas* in the heart,
establishing the vital force of the self in the head,
    thus establishing the concentration of yoga,

"Om," the Brahman of a Single Syllable

(13) pronouncing "*Om*,"

    the *brahman* of a single syllable,

  and meditating on Me,

then when he goes out, leaving the body,

  he arrives at the supreme goal.

Meditating on Krishna

(14) Whoever meditates on Me continually,

  his thoughts not wandering to any other object,

for him, always disciplined

  and holding to his discipline,

  I am easy to attain.

They Are Not Reborn

(15) These great spirits who have come to Me,

  having attained the highest perfection,

they do not go to rebirth,

  that realm of suffering and impermanence.

Existence in Heaven Is Impermanent

(16) As for the world of Brahmā,

  such worlds are subject to continuing rebirth,

but no rebirth is to be had

  by those who have come to Me.

(16) Impermanence of existence in even the highest heaven. "The world of Brahmā" referred to here is the highest heaven of traditional Indian cosmology. But as this passage indicates, existence after death in even the highest heaven (or the lowest hell) lasts only until the finite results of one's actions on this earth are exhausted. The passage which follows **(17–19)** outlines the cosmogony and the larger cosmology of the Indian tradition as interpreted by the *Bhagavad Gītā*.

"The Night and Day of Brahman"

(17) Those people know what night and day are

    who know the "Day of Brahman"

    as including a thousand ages (*yugas*)

and the "Night of Brahman"

    as including a thousand ages.

(18) At the beginning of an eon (*ahaḥ*, "day")

    of existence,

    all phenomenal manifestations

    proceed from the Unmanifest (*avyakta*),

and at the end of an eon (*rātri*, "night"),

    all these phenomena disappear into the Unmanifest

    from which they came.

(19) Coming into existence again and again,

    that same multitude of beings

    passes out of existence at the end of an eon,

only to come into existence again

    at the beginning of a new eon.

(17–19) The Day and Night of Brahman—coming into existence and passing out of existence, over and over again. This is a cyclical conception of the existence and "nonexistence" of the universe, but we must note two things: it is not the "eternal recurrence" of Friedrich Nietzsche, because though "that same multitude of beings" returns at the beginning of an eon, it takes up where it left off when it went out of existence at the end of the previous eon. *Pralaya*, the "passing out of existence" of the universe, is thus a kind of unconsciousness (or sleep) rather than a complete state of nonexistence. It is a temporary, if age-long, "Night of Brahman," not a destruction of the universe, since as we know from Chapter Two, for the metaphysics of the Gītā nothing that exists can ever cease to exist.

A Higher Unmanifest Being

(20)   But higher than this is another Unmanifest being

       which is everlasting

and which does not cease to exist

       when all creatures disappear

       at the end of an eon.

The Supreme Goal, Krishna's Own Highest State

(21)   This Unmanifest is called the Imperishable

       and the highest goal;

attaining That, they do not return—

       That is My own highest state.

To Be Attained by Selfless Devotion

(22) This highest goal

> is the supreme Spirit (*puruṣaḥ paran*),
>
> which is to be attained
>
> by the strictest devotion.

All creatures are grounded in this Being,

> and It is present throughout every one of them.

(20–22) Krishna's own highest state the supreme goal. Here Krishna's own high state of being is declared to be higher even than that of *brahman* (the lower Unmanifest), and it is characterized in the terms earlier used to identify the one transcendent-immanent Reality which is identical with the supreme Self, here referred to as the "supreme Spirit." Note too that this highest goal is to be attained by the "strictest devotion" to deity, *bhakti* yoga, the discipline most easily directed to the highest state of Krishna as goal.

Times and Manner of Dying

(23) I shall now proclaim those times of dying

> at which disciplined persons
>
> depart only to return again

and those times at which they do not return.

The Cycles of Existence and Nonexistence

(24) Firelight, brightness, daylight,
> the bright period of the moon,
> the six months of the northward passage
> of the sun—

dying at these times,
> people who know *brahman* go to *brahman*.

(25) Smoke, night, the dark period of the moon,
> as well as in the southward passage of the sun—

dying at these times,
> the disciplined person returns,
> having attained only to the light of the moon.

(26) These two paths, the light and the dark,
> are said to be everlasting for this world;

by the one, a man goes to the place
> from which there is no return,
> and by the other he returns again.

(27) Whatever fruit of meritorious action
> is decreed in the Vedas for the sacrifices,
> for acts of austerity,
> and also for acts of charity,

he who knows this goes beyond all these
> and arrives at the highest, supreme state.

(23–27) Traditional lore concerning death and dying. Both these passages concerning propitious and unpropitious times for dying and the earlier passages about the last thoughts at the time of death are from traditional conceptions of such matters, probably even earlier than the passages in the *Chandogya Upanisad* from which they are taken.

9

Manifestations of Krishna's Deity

Synthesis of Jnāna and Vijnāna

The Blessed Lord said:

(1) Since you do not argue,

    I shall now proclaim to you

    this highest secret,

this synthesis (*sahitam*, "conjunction")

    of knowledge (*vijnāna*) and wisdom (*jnāna*),

    having known which you will be freed from all evil.

(2) This is the royal science (*rājavidyā*),

    the royal secret, the ultimate purifier—

righteous, undying, directly understandable,

    easy to practice.

(1–2) Bhakti yoga: synthesis of knowledge and wisdom. Here the *Bhagavad Gītā* tells us that the discipline of selfless devotion to deity is to be understood as a "synthesis of knowledge and wisdom," an integration of the necessary philosophical knowledge, *vijnāna*, and the direct unitive knowledge, *jnāna*, of those who are truly wise, that *jnāna* which is held to be the essence of the experience of the one transcendent-immanent Reality. The Gītā here also gives its reasons for holding that the discipline of devotion is to be preferred by most human beings—it is "righteous, undying, directly understandable, easy to practice."

Those without Faith in This Teaching

(3) Men without faith in this teaching (*dharma*)

    do not attain to Me,

returning instead to the cycle of births and deaths.

Krishna as Lord Is Both Immanent and Transcendent

(4) The entire universe is permeated by Me

    in My unmanifest form,

and all creatures are grounded in Me,

    though I am not contained by them.

(5) Yet creatures are not grounded in Me!

Behold My lordly yoga:

    though not contained by creatures,

    I Myself am the cause and support

    of everything that exists.

(6) As the great wind that pervades all places everywhere

    dwells everlastingly in boundless space,

just so all creatures dwell in me—

    you can be certain of this.

(4–6) Krishna as Lord of the universe both transcendent and immanent. The very being and existence of creatures are "grounded in" Krishna as supreme Spirit, but, the Gītā tells us, creatures are not really grounded in him because they "dwell in" the Lord much as the wind

Manifestations of Krishna's Deity

permeates "boundless space." The point of this passage is simply that Krishna as Lord of the universe is both absolutely transcendent of all things and totally immanent within them.

The "Creation" of All Creatures

(7) At the end of an eon

    all creatures depart

    into My primordial Nature (*prakṛti*),

and I send them forth again

    at the beginning of a new eon.

(8) With My own Nature as foundation

    and by means of that Nature's power,

I send forth again and again

    this entire multitude of powerless creatures.

Krishna's Nature the Source of All Things

(10) With Me as Overseer,

    primordial Nature sends forth

    both what moves and what does not move—

the world turns as a result

    of this original cause.

(7–10) Krishna as cause of the cycles of existence and "nonexistence." Here the Gītā again presents its conception of the cyclic existence and "nonexistence" of the universe. But it now elaborates Krishna's part, as Lord of the universe, in these economic processes, for he is said to be the original cause of them.

(11) Fools degrade Me who have taken on human form,
 not knowing My supreme state
   as great Lord of the universe (*lokamaheśvara*).

(12) Vain are their hopes, vain their actions,
   vain their knowledge;
 mindless, they dwell in their ogreish and
   demonic nature, completely deluded.

(13) But those great spirits
   who dwell in the divine Nature,
 they revere Me with unfaltering consciousness,
   knowing Me as the imperishable
 source of all creatures.

(14) Always magnifying Me
   and working with firm resolution,
 giving reverence to Me by means of devotion,
   always disciplined, they worship Me.

By Means of the Sacrifice of Knowledge

(15) Still others worship me
   by means of the sacrifice of knowledge,
 worshipping Me both in My oneness
   and in My various omnipresent manifestations.

Krishna's Many Manifestations

(16) I am the rite,

    I am the Sacrifice,

    I the offering to the ancestors,

    I the medicine.

I am the sacred phrase (*mantram*),

    I am even the purified butter of the offering,

    I am the sacred fire,

    I the sacred oblation.

(17) I am the Father and the Mother

    of this entire universe, the founder, the grandfather,

the object of knowledge, the purifying One,

    the syllable "*Om*,"

    and the *Rig*, *Sāma*,

    and *Yajur Vedas*;

(18) the ultimate goal, the support,

    the witness, the home,

    the place of refuge,

    and the Friend;

the coming into existence,

    the passing out of existence,

    the substance, the storehouse,

    and the undying seed.

(19) I am heat;

    I restrain the rains and send them forth,

I am both death and deathlessness,

    both what exists

    and what does not exist.

(20) Those who are purified of their sins,

    those who know the three Vedas,

    they worship Me with the Sacrifice,

    seeking heaven as their goal;

attaining to the merited world

    of the chief of deities,

    they experience the divine pleasures

    of the deities in heaven.

Existence in the Highest Heaven Is Impermanent

(21) After enjoying the great realm of this heaven,

    when their deeds are exhausted,

    they re-enter the world of men;

holding to the righteousness of the three Vedas

    in this manner, such men,

    craving the satisfaction of their desires,

    attain only what comes and goes.

Krishna's Devotees Get Eternal Peace

(22) Those people who worship Me,

> meditating on Me without any other thought in mind,

if they persevere continually,

> I give them the attainment
>
> and the possession of total peace.

(16–22) Transcendence and immanence of Krishna as great Lord of the universe. In this chapter, the absolute transcedence and total immanence of Krishna are employed to explain the Gītā's continuing insistence on the importance of selfless devotion to deity, as in the long passage just completed. Throughout chapters nine, ten, and eleven, the Krishna-theism of the *Bhagavad Gītā* is elaborated in detail. But as important as this Krishna-theism is, it is not exclusive of other theisms or devotion to other deities, as the passage which follows indicates.

Devotees of Other Deities

(23) Those devotees of other deities

> who worship them with complete faith,

it is I alone

> that even they worship,
>
> though not in the ordained manner.

Krishna the Lord of All Worship

(24) For I am both the object
    and the Lord of all acts of worship.
But those people do not recognize Me
    in the proper manner—
    thus they fall away

(25) Devotees of the deities
    go to the deities,
    devotees of the Fathers
    go to the Fathers,
    worshippers of spirits
    go to the spirits—
but those who worship Me come to Me.

The Spirit of True Worship

(26) Whoever offers Me a leaf,
    a flower, a fruit, or even water,
    with devotion,
such an offering I accept
    from one who is truly devout.

Offer All Actions to the Lord

(27) Whatever you do,

    whatever you eat,

    whatever you give in charity,

    whatever austerity you practice,

do that as an offering to Me.

And Be Liberated from Bondage to All Actions

(28) In this way you shall be freed

    from the bonds of that action

    which produces good and evil fruits.

You shall then come to Me liberated,

    your self integrated

    in the yoga of true renunciation.

Krishna the Same to All Creatures

(29) I am the same to all creatures—

    I neither reject nor favor anyone.

But all who worship Me with devotion are in Me,

    and I also am in them.

. . . Even the Doer of Great Evil

(30) If even a doer of great evil worships Me

    with single devotion,

he must be judged a good man,

    for he has rightly resolved,

(31) and quickly he himself becomes righteous,

    and he then goes to eternal peace.

No Devotee of Krishna Is Ever Lost

You must be sure of one thing:

    no devotee of Mine is ever lost.

(30–31) The wicked as devotee of Krishna. At first glance, these last two *shlokas* seem to say that the universal righteousness of *dharma* can be violated with impunity by a devotee of the Lord. A closer examination of the passage, however, reveals the fact that according to the Gītā, the "doer of great evil . . . must be judged to be a good man" not because his evil deeds are cancelled by his devotion or by Krishna's grace but because "quickly he himself becomes righteous." The evil acts of such a person will still bear fruit, but his new-found righteousness will enable him to counter his old evil ways with the good deeds of his new way of life.

Krishna Accepts All as his Devotees

(32) For if people resort to Me,

    even those of low birth—

    women, *vaiśyas*, and *śūdras* also—

all of them then attain the highest goal.

(33) How much more, then, pure Brahmins

    and devoted warriors and princes!

Having come into this unhappy, impermanent world,

    you should worship Me—

(34) keep your mind on Me,
   be devoted to Me,
   worship and pay reverence to Me!
Having disciplined yourself in this manner,
   with Me as your supreme goal,
   to Me alone shall you come.

10

Krishna as the Cosmic Source of All Things

The Blessed Lord Said:

(1) Now hear yet again My supreme teaching,
which I shall now proclaim to you
> because you are beloved
> and I desire your welfare.

Krishna the Source of All the Deities

(2) Neither the multitudes of deities
> nor even the great sages
> know My origin,

for I am the source
> of all the deities
> as well as of the great sages.

(3) Whoever, undeluded, knows Me
> as birthless and sourceless,
> the great Lord of the universe,

he among mortals is liberated
> from all evils.

Krishna's Powers All-inclusive

(4) Intelligence, wisdom, freedom from delusion,
   patience, truth, control,
   peace, pleasure, pain, coming into existence,
passing out of existence,
   both fear and fearlessness,

(5) harmlessness, equanimity, satisfaction,
   austerity, honor, and disgrace—
however different from one another they may be,
   all the conditions of creatures
   come into existence from Me.

(6) The seven great sages of ancient times
   as well as the four Manus originated from Me,
   as progeny of My mind,
from Whom came forth all
   these creatures in this world.

(7) Whoever knows the essential truth
   of this powerful yoga and product of Mine,
he is disciplined with an unfaltering discipline—
   of this there is no doubt.

Krishna the Source of All Things

(8) I am the source of everything;

> all things come from Me.

Knowing this, enlightened men filled with devotion

> worship Me.

Krishna's Devotees

(9) With their consciousness (*citta*) on Me,

> with their vital force on Me,

they get satisfaction and joy in talking about Me,

> edifying one another.

(10) To them, worshipping Me with love,

> always disciplined,

I give that discipline of the *buddhi*

> by means of which they come to Me.

(11) Showing compassion to these same persons,

> I dispel ignorance born of *tamas-guna*,

dwelling in My own state

> of illuminating knowledge.

Krishna as the Cosmic Source of All Things

Arjuna Extols Krishna's Greatness

Arjuna said:

(12) You are the great purifier,
    the supreme *brahman*,
    the highest state of being!
The deathless, divine Spirit,
    primordial deity, birthless Lord,

(13) all the sages declare You to be,
    as well as the divine sages
    Narada and Asita, Devala, and Vyasa too—
and You Yourself have told me this!

(14) all this that You tell me
    I believe to be true,
for neither the deities nor the demons
    know Your manifestations.

(15) You alone know Yourself
    by means of Your very Self—
supreme Spirit, cause of the existence of creatures,
    Lord of all creatures, deity of deities,
    Lord of the universe!

Arjuna Asks for an Explanation of the Manifestations of Krishna

(16) I therefore pray You to tell me,

    without holding anything back,

    what are those manifestations

    permeating the three worlds

    by means of which You exist forever,

for wonderful indeed

    are all Your transcendent manifestations.

(17) How can I know You,

    how can I always mediate on You—

    You of the great yoga?

And according to what various states of being

    am I to think of You?

(18) Explain, then, in complete detail,

    Your own great, powerful Yoga

    and its transcendent manifestations,

for I am not yet satisfied

    as I listen to Your sweet words.

(16–18) Krishna's transcendent manifestations. Arjuna's request for an explanation of Krishna's many "transcendent manifestations" begins the Gītā's introduction to Chapter Eleven, where Krishna shows himself to Arjuna in all his cosmic and supracosmic forms. Here in Chapter Ten, however, he simply tells Arjuna of his many powers, perfections, and "principal manifestations."

138   *Krishna as the Cosmic Source of All Things*

Krishna All-inclusive

The Blessed Lord said:

(19) Come, then, and since My own
   manifestations are divine,
   I will tell about the principal ones—
but there is no real end to My inclusiveness.

Beginning, Middle, and End of All

(20) I am the Self that dwells
   in the heart of all creatures;
I am the beginning, middle, and end of all beings.

The "Principal Manifestations"

(21) Of heavenly deities (*adityānam*), I am Vishnu,
   of great lights, the bright sun,
of storm deities (*marutam*), I am Marichi,
   of stars, I am the moon.

(22) Of Vedas, I am the *Sama Veda*,
   of the great deities (*devanam*), I am Indra,
of the senses, I am *manas*,
   and I am the *buddhi* of all creatures.

(23) Of the Rudras, I am Shiva,
   of spirits and demons, I am the Lord of wealth,
of the Basus, I am Agni,
   of great mountains, I am Meru.

Krishna as the Cosmic Source of All Things

(24) Of household priests, know that I am Brihaspati,
> the Lord of them all;
of warlords, I am the deity of war (*Skandaḥ*),
> and of the seas, I am the great Ocean.

(25) Of the great sages, I am Bhrigu,
> of *mantras*, I am the single-syllabled "*Om*,"
of acts of sacrifice, I am the repetition
> of the *mantra*, of the great mountain ranges,
I am the Himalayas.

(26) Of all the trees, I am the Ashvatta,
> of heavenly sages, Narada,
of heavenly musicians, the foremost,
> of the perfected ones, the sage Kapila.

(27) Of horses, know Me as Indra's Uchaiḥshravas,
> born from the cosmic nectar,
of royal elephants, Indra's Airavata,
> and of men, I am the ruler.

(28) Of weapons, I am Indra's thunderbolt,
> of cows, I am the Cow of Good Fortune;
I am the fertile deity of love, Kandarpa,
> and of the serpents, I am King Vasuki.

(29) Of the legendary serpents, I am Ananta,
  the endless one,
  of creatures of the water,
  I am their deity, Varuna,
 of the Fathers, I am Aryaman,
  of conquerors, I am Yama, lord of Death.
(30) Of the demons, I am King Prahlada;
  I am ever-compelling Time.
 Of animals, I am Lord of the animals,
  of birds, I am the son of Garuda.
(31) Of purifiers, I am the wind,
  of warriors, I am Rāma,
 of great water dwellers, I am the great Fish,
  of rivers, I am the Ganga.

Krishna the Beginning, Middle, and End of the Universe

(32) I am the beginning and the end
  of the universe,
  and I am the middle also;
 of knowledge, I am knowledge of what
  pertains to the Self,
  and of those who speak, I am speech.

(33) Of the letters, I am the letter 'A',

    and also the duality of compound letters;

I alone am deathless Time,

    I am the Founder,

with faces in every direction.

(34) I am Death who carries everything away,

    as well as the source of everything that exists;

of female beings, I am Fame,

    Good Fortune, and Speech,

    Memory, Wisdom, Strength of Purpose,

and Patience.

(35) Of sacred chants, I am also the great Sama (Veda),

    of sacred verses, I am the Gayatri,

of months, I am the first,

    of seasons, flowering Spring.

(36) I am the gambling of gamblers,

    I am the glory of those who are glorious;

I am victory,

    I am firm resolution,

    I am the courage of those who are courageous.

Krishna Vasudeva in This Incarnation

(37) Of the clan of the Vrishnis,
>I am the son of Vasudeva,
>of the sons of Pandu,
>I am Arjuna,

and of recluses, I am Vyasa,

(38) I am the rod of those who punish,
>I am the statesmanship of those who rule,

and I am the silence of those things
>which are secret; I am the wisdom of the wise.

(39) Furthermore, I am that
>which is the seed of all creatures;

there is nothing whatever,
>no being either moving or immobile,
>that could ever exist without Me.

(40) There is indeed no end
>to My wonderful manifestations;

but I have now given illustrations
>of the inclusiveness of My manifestations;

(41) whatever being manifests either power
>or strength of purpose,

you should know that in every instance
>it originates from a single tiny bit
>of My all-pervading power.

Krishna as the Cosmic Source of All Things 143

What Can All This Mean to a Human Being?

(42) But even after this detailed teaching,
> what can it mean to you?

Supporting this entire universe
> with but a single particle of Myself,

> I remain unmoved.

11

Arjuna's Vision of the Cosmic Krishna

Arjuna's Response to Krishna

Arjuna said:

(1) These words You have spoken
    as a favor to me,
    explaining the highest secret
    concerning the Self;
with these words,
    this my delusion has been dispelled.

(2) For of the existence and perishing of creatures,
    I have heard from You in great detail,
and of Your everlasting greatness of Self as well.

(3) In this manner
    You proclaim Yourself supreme Lord—
I therefore wish to see Your form as deity,
    O supreme Spirit!

(4) Lord, if you think I can see It,
then show Your undying Self to me,
    O Lord of yoga.

The Blessed Lord said:

(5) Then behold My forms
    in the hundreds and thousands,
of various wonderful kinds
    and various colors and shapes!

(6) Behold the Ādityas, the Vasus, the Rudras,
    the two Ashvins, and the Maruts as well—
behold many wonders never seen before!

(7) Here today behold the entire universe
    brought together in My body,
    with both what moves and what does not move,
as well as whatever else you would like to see.

A Divine Eye Is Necessary

(8) But you cannot see Me
    with your own vision;
I therefore give you the divine eye—
    now behold My great power as Lord!

Krishna's Forms as Reported by Sanjaya

Sanjaya said:

(9) Then, O King, having spoken in this manner,
    Krishna, the great Lord of yoga,
revealed his supreme form to Arjuna.

(10) With many mouths and many eyes,
> with many divine attributes,

with many wonderful ornaments,
> and with many divine weapons raised,

(11) clothed in beautiful garlands and divine raiment,
> with heavenly perfumes and unguents,

composed of all marvels,
> the infinite deity,
>> his faces turned in every direction.

(12) If a thousand suns blazed forth
> with light all at once,

that would be like the brilliance of the Great One.

The Entire Universe in Krishna's Body

(13) Then Arjuna beheld the entire universe
> brought together and divided
>> over and over again

in the body of the Deity of Deities.

(14) Filled with awe, his hair standing on end,
Arjuna bowed his head to the Deity
> and, with a sign of reverence, spoke.

Arjuna said:

(15) I see all the deities in Your body, O Lord—
    and multitudes of the various
    kinds of creatures also:
the great Brahmā sitting on his lotus seat,
    and the great sages,
    and the divine serpents too.

(16) I see You with many arms, bellies, mouths, and eyes—
    form without end in every direction;
nor do I see any end, middle,
    or even a beginning to You,
    O Lord of all forms and Lord of all!

(17) I see you with crown, mace, and discus,
    difficult to gaze upon,
a mass of brilliance, bright on all sides,
    with an infinite glory of burning fire
    and sun in every direction.

(18) You are the Imperishable,

    the supreme goal of knowledge;

    You are the final support

    and end of this universe;

You are the deathless Protector

    of the everlasting righteousness (*dharma*);

    I know You to be the primordial

    Person (*puruṣa*).

(19) Beginningless, without middle or end,

    infinitely powerful,

    with innumerable arms,

    your eyes the sun and the moon,

I see You Whose face is blazing fire,

    consuming this entire universe

    with Your brilliance.

(20) This realm between heaven and earth

    is pervaded by You alone in every direction;

beholding this Your marvelous, terrible form,

    the three worlds quake,

    O great Spirit (*mahātma*)!

(21) Now these hosts of deities are going into You;
> some, frightened, press their hands together
> and praise You!

Rank upon rank of great seers
> and perfected ones cry 'Hail!'
> and honor You with many praises.

Deities and Heavenly Beings Enter Krishna

(22) Rudras, Ādityas, Vasus, and *sādhyas*,
> the all-deity (*viśvedeva*)
> Ashvins, Maruts, and the Father,

great gatherings of heavenly
> musicians, spirits, demons,
> and perfected ones gaze on You,
> and all are greatly amazed.

(23) O great-armed One, Your mighty form
> with many mouths and eyes,
> many arms, legs, and feet,

many bellies, many sharp, terrible tusks—
> seeing this, the world trembles,
> and so do I!

(24) Burning in many colors, You touch the sky,
> with wide-open mouths and great burning eyes.

Seeing You in this way, my inmost self trembles,
> and, O Vishnu, I find no stability or peace!

(25) Your mouths are horrible with those great tusks;
    as soon as I see them,
    like the world-devouring fire of Time,
I no longer know where the sky is,
    and I can find no place to hide—
    Lord of the deities, You in Whom
    the universe dwells,

Krishna Devours the Warriors of Both Sides

(26) All those sons of Dhritarashtra,
    along with great numbers of kings—
Bhima, Drona, as well as that son
    of the charioteer (Karna),
    and our own great warriors too,

(27) they hurry into Your mouths,
    horrible and terrifying with their great tusks;
some of them are stuck between the tusks
    and can be seen with their heads crushed.

(28) Just as the many swollen floods of the rivers
    run madly into the great ocean,
so those heroes of this world of man
    enter into Your blazing mouths.

(29) As moths with the greatest urgency
> hurry into a burning flame
>
> to their destruction,

just so the worlds also rush to their destruction
> in Your mouths.

(30) You lick them up in all directions,
> all those worlds,
>
> and devour them with Your blazing mouths;

Your terrible wonders burn, O Vishnu,
> filling the entire universe with brilliance!

Arjuna Asks, "Who Is Krishna?"

(31) Tell me Who You are,
> in this awe-inspiring form—
>
> homage to You! Have mercy on Me!

I wish to know You, the primordial One,
> for I do not understand Your purposes.

Arjuna's Vision of the Cosmic Krishna

Krishna Is Time

The Blessed Lord said:

(32) I am Time, the cause of the ceasing to exist
> of the universe,
>> fully prepared, ready to take in
>> the worlds here.

> Even without you, none of the warriors
>> who are gathered in opposition
>> will continue to live.

(33) Therefore arise and win glory,
>> conquer your enemies
>> and enjoy a prosperous rule;

> these warriors have already been killed long ago
>> by Me Myself—
>> you are merely the instrument.

(34) Drona and Bhīsma and Jayadratha and Karna too,
>> as well as other hero-warriors—
>> kill them!

> They are already killed by Me—
>> do not hesitate, fight!

> You will conquer your enemies in the battle.

(32–34) Krishna as All-devouring Time. As bloodthirsty as these three *shlokas* seem, we must remember two things: (1) The epic setting of the *Bhagavad Gītā* demands that Arjuna learn his painful duty, for the epic requires that he must, in the end, get up and do his duty, which, for a warrior-prince, is to fight in the righteous cause which is his. And (2) we must note that Krishna here identifies himself as "Time" (*kālā*), the ultimate slayer (but not destroyer) of all creatures now living. It is as Time, therefore, that Krishna may be said to have killed all these warriors now ready for battle and that Arjuna may be said to be merely the instrument of their deaths. Krishna concludes by telling Arjuna that he will be the victor in the great battle which is about to begin. Arjuna, however, is still reluctant to do his duty as a warrior.

Sanjaya said:

(35) Hearing these words from Krishna, trembling,

    Arjuna bowed down and spoke

    once again to Krishna,

stammering, greatly afraid,

    and bowing low.

Arjuna said:

(36) It is proper, Krishna, that in praise of You

    this world rejoices

    and is exceedingly happy,

that the demons scatter in all directions, terrified,

    and all the multitudes of perfected ones

    revere You.

(37) And why should they not pay reverence to You,
>great Spirit?
>You are the primordial Creator (*ādikartre*),
>even greater than *brahman*;
>
>O infinite Lord of the deities,
>in Whom dwells the universe,
>You are the Imperishable One,
>all that exists,
>that which does not exist,
>and all that transcends both!

(38) You are the primordial Deity,
>the primordial Person,
>You are the highest support
>and dwelling-place of the universe;
>
>You are the Knower,
>the object of knowledge,
>and the highest state of being (*dhāma*);
>O You of the infinite form,
>the universe is permeated by You!

Krishna Is Various Deities and Heavenly Beings

(39) You are Vāyu, Yama, Agni,
> Varuna, the moon, Prajāpati,
> and the great primordial Father;

Homage! Homage to You a thousand times,
> and yet again let there be even greater homage!

Homage to You!

(40) Homage to You
> from before and from behind,
> homage to You on all sides,
> You Who are All!

O You of endless power, Your skill is immeasurable;
> You have achieved everything—
> therefore You are All!

Arjuna Apologizes to Krishna

(41) Whatever I have foolishly said to You
> through carelessness
> or even from love,

thinking of You as my best friend,
> calling You 'Krishna,' 'Yadava,' 'Friend,'
> not having known this Your greatness;

Arjuna's Vision of the Cosmic Krishna

(42) and if I have treated You disrespectfully,

   making fun of you as we were playing,

   resting, sitting down, or eating,

  either by ourselves or in the presence of others,

   for this I ask Your pardon, O immeasurable One.

(43) You are the Father

   of the world of things that move

   and those that do not move,

   and You are its worshipped,

   most revered Teacher.

  There is none other like You

   throughout the three worlds—

   how then could there be one greater,

   O You of incomparable greatness?

(44) Bowing down and laying my body before You,

   I therefore pray Your grace, O revered Lord;

  as father to son, as friend to friend,

   as lover to beloved,

   please grant mercy, O Deity!

(45) Having beheld what was never before seen,
> I am in ecstasy,
> and yet my heart trembles with fear;
> show me, O Deity, show me now Your old form—
> have mercy, Lord of the deities,
> home of the universe!

Arjuna Asks to See Krishna's Familiar Human Form

(46) I now wish to see You
> wearing Your diadem,
> with Your mace and discus in hand;
>
> please show Yourself
> in the familiar four-armed form,
> You of the universal form!

The Blessed Lord said:

(47) By granting this grace to you, Arjuna,
> this supreme form has been shown
> by My own mysterious yoga-power;
> this form of Mine—
> marvelous, universal, unending, primordial,
>
> which has never before been seen
> by any other than you.

This Grace Granted by Krishna Only

(48) Not by means of the Vedas
> or by acts of worship or study
>
> or giving, nor yet by ritual acts
>
> or by hard austerities

can I be seen in this form
> in the world of man
>
> by any other than you.

(49) Do not be afraid,
> do not be bewildered
>
> at beholding this awe-inspiring form of Mine;

give up your fear, let your heart be cheerful—
> now behold again that same familiar
>
> form of Mine!

Sanjaya said:

(50) Having spoken in this manner to Arjuna,
> Krishna revealed once again his own human form—

and so the Great one (*mahātma*) comforted
> Arjuna in his fear
>
> by taking on again his old friendly form.

Arjuna said:

(51) Seeing now Your kindly human form,

    I am again possessed of My senses

and restored to my usual state.

The Blessed Lord said:

(52) That form of Mine, extremely difficult to see,

    which you have seen,

even the deities continually long

    for the sight of that form.

(53) Neither by means of the Vedas

    nor by means of austerity,

    nor yet by means of the Sacrifice,

may I be seen in that form

    as you have seen Me.

Krishna Can Be Seen in his Cosmic Form by Means of Devotion

(54) For I can be seen in this form

    only by means of unfaltering devotion,

thus to be seen and known

    in the essential truth

    and so entered into.

(55) Doing My work, putting Me first, devoted to Me,

freed from attachment, enemy to no creature—

whoever is like this comes to Me.

(51–55) So ends Arjuna's vision of Krishna in his cosmic form. The awe-inspiring and terrifying experience had rendered Arjuna both ecstatic and fearful; but when Krishna assumes his old familiar four-armed form, Arjuna is reassured. Note that the chapter ends with Krishna reminding Arjuna (and the reader) that devotion to deity is the only means by which his cosmic form may be seen, thus confirming once again the singular importance, for the *Bhagavad Gītā*, of the yoga of selfless devotion.

12

Unitive Knowledge and Selfless Devotion

Arjuna said:

(1) Those devotees, always disciplined,
> who worship You in this manner,

and those who worship
> the indestructible Unmanifest (*brahman*)—
> which of these understands yoga better?

The Yoga of Devotion Is Better

The Blessed Lord said:

(2) With the mind (*manas*) concentrated on Me,
> those who worship Me with unending devotion,
> filled with supreme faith,

these I hold to be most disciplined.

(3) But those who worship
> the imperishable, inexpressible Unmanifest—

omnipresent, unthinkable, immovable,
> changeless, eternal—

(4) controlling the crowd of senses,

> with evenness of mind (*buddhi*)
>
> toward all creatures,

Delighting in the Welfare of All

they also attain to Me only,

> delighting in the welfare
>
> of all creatures.

Attainment of Brahman More Difficult

(5) Greater labor is necessary

> for those who have their minds (*cetasām*)
>
> set on attaining the Unmanifest,

for embodied selves attain that transcendent goal

> with great difficulty.

(6) But those who worship Me,

> giving up all their actions to Me,

concentrating on Me, meditating on Me

> with unwavering discipline,

(7) their minds firmly fixed on Me,

for these I quickly become their Savior

> from the ocean of death and rebirth.

(5–7) The difficulty of attaining brahman. Both the devotees of Krishna as deity and those who attain *brahma-nirvāna*, the unitive experience of the unmanifest *brahman*, are possessed of the highest human good. *Brahman* is usually said to be attained by unitive knowledge (*jnāna*), the most difficult of the disciplines to practice to perfection; and it is for this reason that the yoga of devotion is said to be much easier than the discipline practiced by those who have their hearts and minds "set on attáining the Unmanifest" *brahman*.

Attainment of Oneness with Krishna

(8) Fix your *manas* on Me only

    making the *buddhi* enter into Me;

in this way you will come to dwell in Me henceforth—

    there is no doubt of this.

(9) But if you are unable to fix your

    consciousness (*cittam*) firmly on Me,

then try to attain Me

    by means of the practice of yoga (*dhyāna yoga*).

(10) If you are not able to practice yoga,

    then be completely devoted to action for Me;

for doing action for My sake,

    you will achieve perfection.

(11) But if you are not able to do even this,

then controlling yourself

    give up attachment

    to the fruit of all your actions.

(12) For knowledge is better than the practice of yoga,

   meditation is better than knowledge,

   and renunciation of the fruits of action

   is better than meditation.

for immediate peace

   is the result of such renunciation.

(1–12) Ranking the various disciplines. At first sight, this last *shloka* seems inconsistent, if not downright contradictory, with the first eleven *shlokas*. But we must understand two things. (1) There can be no doubt that here the selfless, disciplined devotion to deity is better when compared with the discipline of the unitive knowledge of *brahman* (2–5). And (2) the *Bhagavad Gītā* often refers to different practices as "best" in specific contexts, just as various teachings, in different contexts, are said to constitute the "highest secret." Apparently in this instance, the discipline of nonattached action or karma yoga is said to be better than the other methods to be resorted to if one cannot practice selfless devotion to deity as prescribed in *shlokas* two and six through eight.

Characterization of the Perfected Yogi

(13) Not rejecting any creature

   always friendly and compassionate,

free from ego and its selfishness,

   patient and evenminded

   in both pleasure and pain,

(14) the integrated (*yukta*) man who is always satisfied,

    who is self-controlled

    and of firm resolution,

whose *manas* and *buddhi* are established in Me,

    such a man is indeed dear to Me.

(15) He before whom no one trembles in fear

    and who is not afraid of others,

who is free from inordinate enjoyment and loathing,

    free from impatience, fear,

    and disturbance of mind,

    he also is dear to Me.

(16) Unworried, pure, skillful,

    without self-interest,

    and free from agitation,

giving up all selfish endeavors

    and devoted to Me,

    such a man is dear to Me.

(17) He who is neither overjoyed nor revolted,

    neither grieves nor craves,

renouncing both good and evil,

    full of devotion,

    he too is dear to Me.

(17) Renunciation of both good and evil. We may be surprised to find Krishna approving the renunciation of both evil and good. What is meant here, though, is renunciation of attachment, positive or negative, to both good and evil, specifically the good and evil fruits of our own and others' actions.

(18) The same to friend and enemy,
      as well as to cold and heat,
      honor and disgrace,

Accepting Both Joy and Sorrow

accepting joy and sorrow alike,
      freed from all attachment,

(19) him to whom blame and praise are the same,
      the man of wisdom,
      content with whatever comes to him,
not attached to his home,
      steadfast of mind
      and filled with devotion,
      such a man is dear indeed to Me!

Those Who Revere This Teaching

(20) Truly, those who revere this teaching
      as it has been proclaimed here,
full of faith and putting Me first,
      those devotees are supremely dear to Me.

13

The Phenomenal Individual Self

Individual Self as "the Field"

The Blessed Lord Said:

(1) This body (*śarīra*) is called "the Field."
Those who know this say that
    whoever knows this Field
    is "the Knower of the Field."

Krishna the Knower of the Field in All Fields

(2) You should understand also
    that I am the Knower of the Field
    in all Fields.
Knowledge of the Field and
    and of the Knower of the Field,
    this I hold to be true knowledge (*jñāna*).

Krishna Explains Knowledge of the Field and Knower of the Field

(3) That field, its characteristics

> as well as what it is,
>
> what its modifications are,
>
> and where each comes from,

as well as Who the Knower of the Field is

> and what His powers are,
>
> that hear from me briefly now.

(4) this has been sung by the sages in many ways

> in each of the various Vedic hymns,

as well as in the precise, fully reasoned words

> of the *Brahma Sūtra*.

(1–4) The Field and the Knower of the Field. This chapter is devoted to an exposition of the nature of the individual human self, here to be known as "the Field." But the individual human being is not only a phenomenal self; he is also the possessor of the supreme Self of all creatures, known here as "the Knower of the Field." This exposition is presented in terms of the *gunas* of *prakriti* with which we are already familiar. But it also attempts a synthesis of Sāmkhya's *prakriti–purusha* dualism and the nondualism (*advaita*) of the Upanishads and the *Brahma Sūtra*. The synthesis is achieved by identifying *purusha* or Spirit with the supreme Self which, in the Upanishads, is identified with *brahman*. "The Knower of the Field" is therefore, in the Gītā's version, both Sāmkhya's *purusha* and the Upanishads' supreme Self (*paramātma*).

Constituents of the Phenomenal Self

(5) The five gross elements,

> ego-consciousness (*ahamkāra*),
>
> the discriminating will (*buddhi*),
>
> and the Unmanifest,

as well as the eleven senses

> and the five objects of sensation;

(6) desire-aversion (*icchādvesa*), pleasure-pain;

> the synthesis (*samgātah*)
>
> of all these constituents;
>
> consciousness (*cetanā*) and firmness
>
> of purpose (*dhṛti*)—

this, in sum, with its modifications,

> is said to constitute the Field.

(5–6) The constituents of the individual human being. Here the *Bhagavad Gītā* provides a summary outline of the basic constituents of the phenomenal individual self. The five gross elements—earth, water, fire, air, and "ether" (*ākāśa*, "the unbounded")—make up the physical body (*deha*). The "Unmanifest" here is not the unmanifest *brahman* of Chapter Twelve but the undifferentiated *prakriti* which constitutes the substance or "matter" of all things. The eleven senses are the usual five senses conceived as five senses turned outward (the sense organs) plus five "inner senses" which convey our sensations to the *manas*, which is therefore the "eleventh sense" and, if functioning properly, the controller of the other senses. Note that the contradictory emotions, "desire-and-aversion," "pleasure-and-pain," are also said to be constituents of the self. But the Gītā interrupts this analysis of the self with an explanation of what constitutes "true wisdom" (*jnāna*) in human affairs.

Nature of True Wisdom in Action

(7) Absence of pride and deceit,

    nonviolence, patience, righteousness,

service of the teacher, purity, self-control;

(8) dispassion in relation to the objects of the senses,

    absence of egotism;

perception of the evils of birth, death, old age,

    disease, and suffering;

(9) nonattachment and freedom from undue affection

    for sons, wife, home, and so on;

everlasting evenness of mind

    when either desirable

    or undesirable things occur;

(10) undeviating in discipline

    and unalterably devoted to Me;

resorting to solitary places

    and aversion to crowds of people;

(11) constantly established in knowledge

> relating to the Self
>
> and apprehending that object of knowledge
>
> which is the essential truth (*tattva*)—

all this is declared to be wisdom (*jnāna*);

> anything other than this is unwisdom.

(11) "Jnāna" as "wisdom". I translate "*jnāna*" as "wisdom" here, even though its usual meaning is simply "knowledge," often "unitive knowlege," and I do so because the passage clearly refers to the results of knowledge in human experience—results in the character and conduct of the man or woman who possess such knowledge.

Knowledge of the Supreme Self as Brahman

(12) I shall now explain

> that object of knowledge
>
> which to know is to attain deathlessness:

the supreme, beginningless *brahman*,

> which is said to be neither
>
> existent nor nonexistent.

(13) With hands and feet everywhere,

> heads, eyes, and mouths turned
>
> in every direction,

hearing from every side throughout the universe

> and moving in every direction,
>
> it yet remains still.

(14) Appearing to have the characteristics
> of all the senses,
> it is nevertheless completely
> different from the senses.

Not attached to anything
> and yet sustaining everything,
> beyond the *gunas* yet experiencing them;

Brahman Both Immanent and Transcendent

(15) being both outside creatures and within them,
> without movement and yet moving,
> both far away and very near,

it is so extremely subtle
> that it is incomprehensible
> (*avijneyam*, "unknowable").

(16) Within all creatures,
> it remains both divided and whole,

and it must be known as both the destroyer
> and the source and sustenance of all beings.

Goal and Object of Knowledge—and That Knowledge Itself

(17) It is also said to be the light of all lights,

> transcending all darkness.

It is that goal of knowledge,

> that object of knowledge,
>
> and that very knowledge itself
>
> which is grounded in the heart of all creatures.

(18) Thus, in sum, the Field as well as knowledge

> and the object of knowledge
>
> have been proclaimed.

Comprehending this,

> a devotee of Mine attains My state of being.

(12–17) The Upanishadic Brahman Characterized. In this passage, the *Bhagavad Gītā* characterizes *brahman*, in the Upanishadic manner, as the absolute, transcendent-immanent One Reality. In this conception of it, *brahman* is said to be that absolute reality (*sat*) which is identical with the supreme Self as absolute consciousness (*cit*). To realize this *brahman*-Self in one's own actual experience is, in this view, the highest human good, that final liberation from birth-and-death which is the ultimate goal of all human existence. Because this *brahman*-Self is conceived as absolute and as infinite (*ananta*, "unending"), its characterization is here more paradoxical than definitive. But note that *brahman* is identified not only as the goal of unitive knowledge but as that very liberating knowledge itself.

"Nature and "Spirit," Prakriti and Purusha

(19) You should know

> that both primordial Nature and Spirit
>
> are without beginning;

and you should know also

> that both the *gunas* and their modifications
>
> originate from *prakriti*,

Prakriti the Source of All Things

(20) which is therefore said to be the source

> of all that acts,
>
> of all instruments of action,
>
> and of all the effects of action as well.

Purusha is the cause of the experience

> of pleasure and pain.

Purusha Experiences the Activity of the Gunas

(21) For so long as *purusha* takes its stand in *prakriti*,

> it experiences the *gunas*
>
> which originate from *prakriti*,

and attachment to the *gunas* is the cause

> of *purusha's* birth from either
>
> good or evil wombs.

(19–21) The dualism of purusha and prakriti. At this point the Gītā seems to leave, at least temporarily, its identification of *brahman* and the supreme Self, for it here presents a complete dualism of Spirit and Nature (or "matter"). We shall soon see, however, that this dualism is not the *Bhagavad Gītā*'s last word concerning the nature of man and the rest of reality, for this dualism of *prakriti* and *purusha* is to be partially resolved by the identification of the "highest Spirit" with the supreme Self (22).

The Highest Purusha Is the Supreme Self

(22) As witness,

>   and as the giver of consent,

>   as supporter, as experiencer,

>   and as the great Lord,

> the supreme Self is also said

>   to be the highest Spirit in this body.

(23) Whoever knows *purusha, prakriti*,

>   and the *gunas* in this manner,

> he is not reborn,

>   whatever his present status may be.

Ways to Knowledge of the Supreme Self

(24) Some perceive the Self

>   within the self with the self

>   by means of meditation-contemplation (*dhyāna*),

> others by discipline of the *buddhi*,

>   and other by means of the yoga

>   of nonattached action.

(25) Still others, not knowing this Self

    but hearing of it from those who do, revere it,

and they also go beyond death

    because of their devotion

    to the divine revelation which they have heard.

(24–25) Ways of getting knowlege of the supreme Self. The four ways of realizing the supreme Self (now identified as the "highest Spirit" or *purusha*) correspond to the four major kinds of yoga: *dhyāna*, the discipline of meditation-contemplation outlined in chapter six; *jnāna*, the discipline of unitive knowledge, which was said to be most difficult; *karma*, the discipline of nonattached action explained in chapters two and three; and *bhakti*, the discipline of selfless devotion to deity.

Conjunction of the Field and the Knower of the Field

(26) Insofar as any being, either mobile or immobile,

    comes into existence,

you should know

    that it is from conjunction (*samyoga*)

    of the Field and the Knower of the Field.

(26) Existence from conjunction of the Field and the Knower of the Field. Here the *Bhagavad Gītā* presents the Sāmkhya philosophy's conception of the origin of all phenomenal existence, telling us that when *purusha* and *prakriti* come into conjunction with one another, *prakriti*, which until then had been undifferentiated and static, becomes activiated, and the three *gunas* which compose *prakriti* lose their equilibrium and become active, which causes the arising of the phenomenal universe, the "three worlds" of the traditional cosmology. Neither the Gītā nor the Samkhya texts explain why this conjunction takes place or why it results in the activation of the undifferentiated *prakriti*.

The Supreme Spirit the Same in All Creatures

27) Whoever sees Him, the supreme Lord,

> dwelling the same in all creatures,

> not dying when they die,

he truly sees.

(28) For seeing the same Lord

> firmly established in all,

he himself does not harm himself in others—

> thus he goes to the supreme good.

All Action Is done by the Gunas Alone

(29) Whoever understands both that

> all actions are done entirely

> by the *gunas* alone

and that the Self is not the doer,

> that man truly understands.

(30) When he perceives the many states of existence

> as established in this oneness

> and their development from that alone,

he then attains *brahman*.

The Self Does Not Act at All

(31) Because it is without beginning

and beyond the *gunas*,

the supreme unalterable Self does not act

even when it dwells in the body,

nor is it contaminated by actions.

Nor Is It Affected by Actions

(32) Just as because of it subtleness

the all-pervading ether

is not contaminated,

just so the Self dwelling in every body

is not contaminated.

(33) Just as the sun alone illuminates this entire world,

just so the Possessor of the Field

illuminates the whole Field.

Knowing This Results in the Supreme Good

(34) Those who know

with the vision of wisdom

this distinction between the Field

and the Knower of the Field,

as well as liberation from the *prakriti*

of creatures,

they go to the supreme good.

14

The Gunas in Human Experience

The Blessed Lord said:

(1) I will now proclaim again that supreme knowledge,
> the ultimate secret,
knowing which all the sages have gone from this world
> to the greatest perfection.

(2) Having resorted to this wisdom
> and having been conformed (*saddharmya*)
> to my Nature,
they do not come to be born
> at the arising of a new eon,
> nor do they suffer
> at the end of an old eon.

Krishna as Activator of Brahman-prakriti

(3) For Me, great *brahman* is the womb
> in which I sow the seed—
the birth of all creatures
> comes from that sowing.

(4) Whatever forms originate in all wombs,

    great *brahman* is the Womb—

I am the Father who provides the seed.

(3–4) Krishna as sower of the seed of the universe. According to the *Bhagavad Gītā*, the phenomenal universe is not created—it is simply the result of an arising (*sarga*, cf. Eng. "surge") out of the undifferentiated *prakriti* activated by conjunction (*samyoga*) with *purusha*, as explained in chapter thirteen. Here, however, Krishna as Lord of the universe is portrayed as the activating Spirit, since he is said to be the ultimate *purusha, purushottama*. Note that here "great *brahman*" is to be identified not with the supreme Self but with the undifferentiated *prakriti* from which the phenomenal universe arises.

The Three Gunas Defined and Explained

(5) *Sattva* (purity, clarity—literally, "beingness"),

    rajas (energy, activity), and *tamas*

    (inertia, dullness)

are the *gunas*, that originate from *prakriti*,

which hold the deathless embodied One to the body.

The Nature of Sattva-guna

(6) Of these, *sattva*, because of its purity,

    is free from evil and is illuminating,

but it binds because attachment to knowledge

    and attachment to happiness result from it.

Rajas-guna

(7) You must understand that *rajas* is
    of the nature of passion (*rāga*),
  which arises from craving and attachment;
it binds the embodied One
    by means of attachment to actions.

Tamas-guna

(8) And you must know that *tamas*
    is born of ignorance,
  the deluder of all embodied beings;
it binds by means of carelessness,
    laziness and sleep.

Effects of the Gunas in Human Experience

(9) Thus *sattva* results in attachment to happiness,
    rajas in attachment to action.
But *tamas*, obscuring knowledge,
    surely results in attachment to carelessness.

Dominance of Each of the Gunas

(10) Sometimes *sattva* prevails over *rajas* and *tamas*,
    sometimes *rajas* overcomes both *sattva* and *tamas*,
and sometimes *tamas* conquers both *sattva* and *rajas*.

Dominance of Sattva

(11) One may know that *sattva* is dominant

when the mind and all the senses

are illuminated by knowledge.

Dominance of Rajas

(12) But when restlessness, greed, craving,

busyness, and the urge to action arise,

rajas is dominant.

Dominance of Tamas

(13) And when dullness, idleness,

carelessness, and delusion arise,

tamas is dominant.

(5–13) The gunas in human nature and experience. Here and in the chapters to follow, the *Bhagavad Gītā* elaborates its teaching concerning the three *gunas* and their effects in human character and experience. In order to understand this metaphysical psychology, we must remember that it is the three *gunas*, their modifications, and their activities which make up the individual nature (*svabhāva*) of every creature and that it is one's own *guna*-nature alone which performs all the actions of the individual self. Note, too, that each of the *gunas*, even the "pure" *sattva-guna*, binds the Self to the body by means of a characteristic attachment.

Dominance of the Gunas at Death

(14) Thus when the embodied One

   dominated by *sattva*

   goes to dissolution at death,

then the individual self goes to the flawless worlds

   of those who possess the highest knowledge.

(15) Going to dissolution dominated by *rajas*,

   he is born among those attached to actions;

and likewise if he goes to dissolution

   dominated by *tamas*,

   he is then born from deluded wombs.

Fruits of Sattvic Actions

(16) They say that the fruit of action

   well done is flawless and of the nature of *sattva*.

. . . of Rajasic and Tamasic Actions

But the fruit of rajasic action

   is suffering, and the fruit

   of tamasic action is ignorance.

Fruits of the Three Gunas

(17) Knowledge is born of *sattva*,

just as greed is born of *rajas*,

and as carelessness, delusion, and ignorance

are born of *tamas*.

(18) Those who are established in *sattva*

go to the heights,

people of *rajas* dwell in the middling places;

caught in the power of the lowest *guna*,

people of *tamas* go to the depths.

We Must Transcend All Three Gunas

(19) When the seer sees no other doer

than the *gunas*,

and when he knows That

which is higher than the *gunas*,

he then attains My state of being.

(20) Transcending these *gunas*

which originate with the body,

the embodied One, liberated

from birth, old age, death,

and suffering, then attains deathlessness.

(14–20) The gunas must be transcended. All actions of whatever kind are done entirely by the *gunas* of one's own individual *guna*-nature, and the *gunas* consequently have the effects noted above on the character and experience of the individual. But the yogi must transcend the *gunas* and all their effects if he is to be liberated from bondage to birth, death, and rebirth. The necessary transcendence is not an attempt to deny or reject the actions of the *gunas*; it is instead an attitude or state of mind characterized by evenness of mind in the midst of all actions, and it is attained by unitive knowledge, meditation-contemplation, or selfless devotion to deity as well as by nonattached action.

How Are the Gunas Transcended?

Arjuna said:

(21) When a man has transcended these three *gunas*,

> by what characteristics is he to be known?

How does he act—

> and how does he get beyond these three *gunas*?

Gunas Transcended by Evenness of Mind

The Blessed Lord said:

(22) He does not reject illumination,

> activity, or even delusion when they arise,

nor does he long for them

> when they have ceased.

'Sitting in' as Though 'Sitting It Out'

(23) Undisturbed by the *gunas*,

    sitting in like one sitting it out,

thinking, 'Only the *gunas* are acting,'

    whoever stays strong and is not moved,

(24) the one for whom pain and pleasure are the same;

    self-reliant, for whom dirt, stones,

    and gold are all the same; strong,

the one for whom blame and praise for himself

    are the same;

(25) the same in both honor and disgrace,

    the same to groups of both friends and enemies,

    giving up all selfish endeavors,

such a man is declared to be *guna*-transcendent.

(21–25) Transcending the gunas by means of acceptance and evenness of mind. In chapter two, the Gītā defined "yoga" as "evenness of mind" and "skill in actions." That evenness of mind is here specified as the means for the transcendence of the *gunas* in the midst of our everyday activities and our everyday emotions. But note once again that evenness of mind is not stoic detachment from action, nor is it a rejection of the vicissitudes of human experience. The yogi who transcends the *gunas* must simply accept them and their activities and effects—the illumination of sattvic activity, rajasic actions, even the delusion of *tamas*; but he accepts them without attachment either positive or negative.

The Gunas in Human Experience

(26) And whoever serves Me
> with the undeviating yoga of devotion
> having transcended the *gunas*,
>
> he is ready to become one with *brahman*,

(27) for, deathless and undying,
> I am the support of *brahman*,
> as well as of both the everlasting
> righteousness (*dharma*).

15

Deity as Both Immanent and Transcendent

Aśvattha, the "World Tree"

The Blessed Lord said:

(1) It is said that the Aśvattha tree is undying,
    its roots above and its branches below,
    its leaves the sacred chants of the Vedas.
Whoever knows this, he is the knower of the Vedas.

(2) Sustained by the *gunas*,
    its branches spreading both downward and upward,
    with the objects of the senses as its trunk,
its roots are also spread out below,
    causing actions here in the world of mankind.

(3) Here in this world,

> it is not understood in this manner,
>
> neither its end nor its beginning
>
> nor its foundation.

This firmly rooted Aśvattha tree

> having been cut down
>
> by the strong axe of nonattachment,

The Yogi Resorts to the Primordial Spirit

(4) that state must then be sought

> to which having gone
>
> men do not return again,

thinking, 'I resort to that same

> primordial Spirit (*ādyam puruṣam*)
>
> from which all this activity
>
> emanated of old.'

(1–4) Not prakriti but purusha must be resorted to for transcendence of the gunas. The myth of the Aśvattha tree is a Vedic myth symbolizing the world and the activity of the *gunas* which constitute all phenomenal reality. Here Krishna teaches that freedom from bondage to that world of actions must be sought by resorting not to the *guna*-nature of the world but to the primordial Spirit which originally caused the arising of phenomenal reality by coming into conjunction with the *prakriti* from which the world of the *gunas* and their activity came.

The "Undying State"

(5) Without pride and without delusion,

    the evil of attachment overcome,

    eternally established in what

    relates to the Self,

    all desires gone,

    liberated from the dualities

    known as pleasure and pain,

such undeluded persons attain that undying state.

(6) The sun does not shine there,

    nor the moon nor fire—

having gone to that place,

    they do not return.

    That is My undying state.

Rebirth of the Individual Self

(7) In the world of living creatures (*jīvaloka*),

    a tiny particle (*aṁśa*) only of Me

    becomes the everlasting individual spirit (*jīva*).

It draws the senses along,

    which are grounded in *prakriti*,

    with *manas* established as the sixth sense.

(8) When He takes on a body,

> as well as when He leaves it,

the Lord moves on, taking them with Him,

> just as the wind carries fragrances

> from their places.

(9) Established in eye, ear, skin, tongue, and nose,

> as well as in *manas*,

He enjoys the objects of the senses.

(10) As He leaves the body

> or as He stays and enjoys,

> accompanied by the *gunas*,

> those who are deluded do not perceive Him;

but those with the eye of wisdom

> are aware of Him.

(11) Yogis working hard at their discipline also see Him

> established in their self;

but deluded men who have not perfected the self

> do not see Him however hard they try.

(7–11) Death and rebirth of the individual self. In Chapter Two, the *Bhagavad Gītā* provided a very simple explanation of its conception of the rebirth of the individual human being—the embodied supreme Self was said to leave the body at death, only to take on another body in a continuing process until final liberation from all birth, death, and rebirth is attained. Here the Gītā elaborates its conception of rebirth, explaining in summary form just what aspects and functions of the individual self are "carried over" to a new life in a new body. In this conception of the process of rebirth, we see that it is the gross physical body alone which perishes at death and that the more "subtle" constituents and functions of the individual remain together to come into existence again as an individual self possessing a new body. We learn here that according to the Gītā it is the senses and the sense-mind, *manas*, which are reborn, and in chapter six (.43) we learned that the *buddhi* is also reborn. The Gītā nowhere tells us explicitly that the ego-consciousness, *ahamkāra*, is reborn, though that it too is reborn may be inferred, as in the passage in Chapter Six referred to above.

The Glory of Krishna

(12) The glorious light that comes from the sun

    which illuminates the world,

        as well as that of the moon and of fire,

know that to be My own glorious light.

Krishna Active and Immanent in All

(13) Permeating both the earth

    and all creatures,

        I sustain them by means of My power (*ojas*);

and having become the sweet Soma plant,

    I also nourish all plants.

Krishna the Life-force of All

(14) Having become the life-force (*vaiśvānara*)

    of all creatures,

    thus seated in the bodies

    of all living beings

    and integrated with their very breathing,

I myself digest their four kinds of food.

Krishna in the Hearts of All

(15) I am seated in the heart of all creatures—

    memory, knowledge, and reasoning come from Me.

I am also what is to be known in the Vedas—

    indeed, I am both the source of the Vedanta

    and the knower of the Vedas.

(13–15) Krishna immanent in all creatures. We learned in chapter seven (.19) that according to the Gītā "Krishna is all"; here the Gītā elaborates Krishna's immanence in all things by saying that by means of his divine power the Lord is the very life of all living creatures.

The "Two Spirits" of This World

(16) Here in this world

    there are two spirits (*puruṣau*),

    one perishable, the other imperishable.

All creatures are perishable,

    but the imperishable Spirit

    is said to be unchanging (*kūtastha*).

A Third "Highest" Spirit

(17)   But there is yet another Spirit, the highest,
    which is called "the supreme Self" (*paramātma*)
This Spirit, the undying Lord,
    enters into the three worlds
    and supports them.

Krishna Is This "Ultimate Spirit"

(18)   Because I transcend the perishable spirit
    and am also higher than the imperishable Spirit
I Myself am therefore declared,
    both in the world and in the Vedas,
    to be the ultimate Spirit (*puruṣottama*).

(19)   The undeluded man who knows Me in this manner
    as the ultimate Spirit,
    he knows all,
and he is therefore devoted to Me
    with his entire being.

This the "Most Secret" Teaching

(20)   Here the most secret doctrine
    has been proclaimed by Me.
Having known this, a man would be truly enlightened
    and would have accomplished
    what should be accomplished.

(16–20) The "three spirits," the supreme Self, and the Lord. Here the *Bhagavad Gītā* presents its final synthesis of the Upanishadic nondualism of *brahman* and the supreme Self on the one hand and the dualism of *prakriti* and *purusha* on the other. The synthesis is achieved, as noted in chapter thirteen (.22), by means of the third and highest Spirit, the "ultimate Spirit" or *purushottama*, which is said to be both immanent in all creatures and transcendent of them. This ultimate Spirit is then identified with the supreme Self and with Krishna as the transcendent-immanent Lord.

16

Divine and Demonic Natures

The "Divine Way"

The Blessed Lord said:

(1) Fearlessness, inner purity,
    persistence in the discipline of knowledge;
generosity, self-control, sacrifice, the study of scripture;
    austerity, righteousness,
(2) nonviolence, truthfulness, nonattachment, peace;
    possession of a mind without guile;
compassion toward all creatures,
    gentleness, and humility;
    unvacillating and free of selfish desires;
(3) possession of dignity without pride;
    patience, firmness of purpose,
    purity, harmlessness—
these are the characteristics of one
    who is born to the divine way of life.

The "Demonic Way"

(4) Hypocrisy, arrogance, egotistical pride,

> anger, violence of speech, and ignorance—

these are the characteristics of one

> who is born to the demonic way of life.

(1–4) Two ways of life—the divine and the demonic. In this chapter the *Bhagavad Gītā* describes the characteristics and qualities of the conduct, character, and consciousness belonging to two kinds of people: those who are born to "the divine way of life" and those who are born to "the demonic way of life." The two ways and the corresponding kinds of people are strongly contrasted, but this twofold analysis is not to be understood as teaching that men and women are the victims or beneficiaries of some "fate" external to themselves and their own actions. The individual human being is always born to his own way of life as the result of his own deliberate actions in previous lifetimes. The value of this chapter is therefore the exposition and description it provides of those characteristics and qualities of character and conduct which should be cultivated and those that are to be avoided.

Way to Liberation and Way to Bondage

(5) The divine way leads to liberation;

> the demonic way is known to lead
>
> to continued bondage.

Do not be grieved:

> you are born with the divine qualities!

Two Kinds of Living Creatures

(6) Two kinds of creatures arise in this world,
> the divine and the demonic.

The divine has been explained in detail;
> now hear from Me the demonic.

"Demonic" People

(7) Demonic people know neither action
> nor the cessation of action.

In them, neither purity nor right action
> nor even truth is to be found.

Nihilists and Atheists

(8) Such people say that there is no truth, no Lord,
> and that the world has no divine foundation
>
> and is without any sustaining order.

They are motivated by nothing
> other than egotistical desire.

(9) Holding stubbornly to this view,
> of little intelligence,
>
> having lost their very selves,

these wicked people come forth
> committing acts of violence
>
> for the destruction of the world.

(10) Holding to an insatiable desire
    and possessed by hypocrisy,
    conceit, and arrogance,
holding to false views
    as a result of their delusion,
    they act for their own impure purposes.

(11) They devote themselves to unending cares
    that last until death;
their highest goal is the enjoyment
    of their desires,
    believing that there is nothing else of value.

(12) Bound by hundreds of ties of craving
    and given wholly to desire and anger,
to satisfy their desires
    they seek hoards of wealth by unlawful means.

(13) "Today I have gained this,
    and I shall also get that other desire;
this is all mine,
    and that treasure is also going to be mine."

(14) "I have killed my enemy over there,
    and I will kill others as well;
I alone am master,
    I am the one who controls all pleasures,
    I am perfect, powerful, and happy;"

Divine and Demonic Natures 203

(15) "I am both wealthy and of high birth—

    who else is equal to me?

    I will offer sacrifice, give gifts, and exult!"

So these people talk,

    deluded by their ignorance.

(16) Confused by a divided consciousness

    and trapped in the web of delusion,

concerned only with the enjoyment of their desires,

    they go down to a foul hell.

(17) Self-important, stubborn,

    filled with the egotism and arrogance of wealth,

they perform the Sacrifice in name only,

    ostentatiously and not in the ordained manner.

(18) These cruel, repulsive, degraded people—

I continually cast such evil ones

    into demonic wombs only,

    throughout the round of existence.

(20) Coming deluded into demonic wombs

    birth after birth,

they do not by any means attain to Me

    but go to the lowest place.

(18–20) Foul hells and birth from deluded wombs. Such people "go to the lowest place" and are reborn again and again from "demonic wombs" not because they are doomed by deity to do so but because they continually refuse to resort to the Lord and to those disciplines which are capable of setting them on the right path. They themselves have rejected the divine way of life, motivated by the egotistical desires born of their stubborn delusion.

Gateway to Hell: Desire, Greed, and Anger

(21) This is the triple gateway to hell

>which destroys the self—

>desire, greed, and anger.

You must give up these three evils.

(22) But liberated from this triple gateway of darkness,

>a man accomplishes the good of the self,

and he thus attains the highest goal.

Obey the Law's Commands

(23) Whoever ignores the Law's commands,

>living according to his own selfish desires,

he attains neither perfection nor happiness

>nor the highest good.

(24) Therefore let the Law (*śāstra*) be your authority

>in deciding what you should and should not do.

Observing what is set down in the Law's commands,

>you should do action here in this world.

(23–24) "The Law's commands." The "Law" referred to here is the traditional injunctions concerning right and wrong action to be found in scriptural texts known as "*shāstras*," texts which specify and interpret scriptural commandments and prohibitions.

17

Actions Correlated with the Gunas

Arjuna said:

(1) But what is the status of those
    who reject the Law's commands
    yet sacrifice with complete faith?
Are such people of *sattva*, of *rajas*, or of *tamas*?

Three Kinds of Faith

The Blessed Lord said:

(2) The faith of human beings is of three kinds,
    each born of the nature of the individual
and characterized either by *sattva*,
    by *rajas*, or by *tamas*—
    listen to this:

As a Man's Faith Is, So Is He Himself

(3) The faith of everyone is correlated

    with his individual nature.

Indeed, the human spirit is made up of faith,

    and as a man's faith is,

    just so is he himself.

(1–3) Human character and the three gunas. Throughout Chapter Seventeen and much of Chapter Eighteen, the *Bhagavad Gītā* elaborates further the nature of human character and conduct in terms of the three *gunas* which compose the individual nature of everyone. Here, for example, faith is said to be the very essence of the human spirit, and that faith is correlated with each of the three *gunas* in relation to the three kinds of worship that are typical of the three kinds of *guna*-nature.

Worship and the Three Gunas

(4) Men of *sattva* worship the deities,

    men of *rajas* worship spirits

    of power and action,

and men of *tamas* worship ghosts

    and other fantastic spirits.

The Practice of Cruel Austerities

(5) People who practice cruel austerities

    not ordained by Law,

made up of hypocrisy and egotism,

    full of desire, passion, and violence;

(6) such fools starve

> the group of constituents within the body—
>
> and even Me Myself
>
> Who am within the body!

Know that such people are of demonic resolution.

(5–6) The demonic practice of cruel austerities. We have seen that the Gītā does not teach or condone the renunciation of all action, which apparently some yogis of the time were wont to attempt; and it rejects these attempts in the strongest of terms, as we have seen. Now we see that the Gītā also rejects the practice of what it refers to as "cruel austerities," practices which, again, some yogis of the time undertook. We learned in Chapter Six that the *Bhagavad Gītā* taught a "middle way" between indulgence and extreme asceticism.

Three Kinds of Diet

(7) But even the good

> of everyone is of three kinds,
>
>> just as are their worship, austerities and gifts.

Listen now to the difference between them.

Sattvic Food

(8) Food that builds life, courage, strength,

> health, happiness, and contentment—

such foods are dear to men of *sattva*.

Rajasic Food

(9) Men of *rajas* desire foods

    which are bitter, sour, salty,

    hot, pungent, or burning,

foods which cause pain, suffering, and illness.

Tamasic Food

(10) Stale, tasteless, putrid, and rotten,

    leftovers, and even impurities—

such food is dear to the man of *tamas*.

(7–10) The sattvic diet. What is interesting in this description of the kinds of food correlated with each of the *guna*-natures is the sensible diet recommended as food "dear to the man of *sattva*"—a diet conducive to both health and happiness. We know that according to the Gītā the yogi should eat with moderation; here we learn that he should enjoy food which produces the health and strength necessary for the practice of his discipline.

Sattvic Worship

(11) Properly ordained worship (*yajna*)

    offered by people not desiring any reward

    and offered with a concentrated mind

    simply because it is considered to be

    one's duty—

such worship is of *sattva*.

Rajasic Worship

(12) But worship offered

    for the purpose of getting a reward

    or from hypocrisy or ostentation,

that worship must be known to be of *rajas*.

Tamasic Worship

(13) Unordained worship,

    with no proper offering of food or money,

    and done without the necessary faith,

such worship is of *tamas*.

Austerity of Body

(14) Homage to the deities, to Brahmins,

    to teachers, and to wise men,

    purity, steadfastness, continence,

    and nonviolence—

these are said to constitute austerity of body.

Austerity of Speech

(15) Words not resulting in conflict,

    true words that are pleasant

    and for the good of those who hear them,

    as well as words recited

    in the study of scriptures—

this is said to constitute austerity of speech.

Austerity of Mind

(16) Tranquility of consciousness,
>gentleness, quietness, self-control,
>and purification of one's nature (*bhava*)—

this is said to be austerity of the mind.

Sattvic Austerity

(17) Performed with supreme faith
>by disciplined men seeking no reward,

this kind of threefold austerity
>they call "sattvic."

Rajasic Austerity

(18) Whatever austerity is done in this world
>to gain respect, honor, and deference,
>and done with hypocrisy,

this kind of austerity is called "rajasic,"
>and it is both impermanent and powerless.

Tamasic Austerity

(19) If austerity is done with delusion of mind,
>by means of self-torture
>or in order to destroy another person,

this kind of austerity is declared to be of *tamas*.

(14–19) Proper austerities of body, speech, and mind. The Gītā rejects "cruel austerities" and "self-torture," but it commends and counsels a proper austerity of "body, speech, and mind," an austerity which is inward rather than ostentatious or for the gaining of personal power.

Sattvic Giving

(20) The gift that is given
> at the right time and place
>
> to one who is worthy of it,
>
> without thought of reward,
>
> simply thinking, "One should give,"

such a gift is known to be of *sattva*.

Rajasic Giving

(21) But whatever is given
> in order to get something in return,
>
> or, again, with the fruit of the action in mind,
>
> or with reluctance,

that gift is said to be of *rajas*.

Tamasic Giving

(22) Whatever gift is given
> at the wrong time and place
>
> to persons not worthy of it,
>
> without signs of respect and with contempt,

that gift is declared to be of *tamas*.

"Om, Tat, Sat"

(23) *"Om, tat, sat"*—
> that is the traditional threefold
> invocation of *brahman*,

by means of which Brahmins
> as well as both the Vedas and acts of worship
> were ordained in ancient times.

(24) After uttering "*Om*," therefore,
> acts of worship, of giving, and of austerity
> are always initiated by knowers of *brahman*,

as ordained by the Vedic injunctions.

(25) Thus with "*tat*"
> and without seeking the fruit,

works of worship, of austerity,
> and of various kinds of giving
> are done by those seeking liberation.

"Sat" Means "Being" and "the Good"

(26) The word "*sat*"
> means both "reality" and "the good,"

and it is also used
> to refer to commendable action.

Actions Correlated with the Gunas

(27) In relation to worship, to austerity,
    and to giving,
    steadfastness is also called "*sat*,"
and action for these purposes
    is called "*sat*" as well.

(28) Thus oblation, gift, austerity,
    and action done without faith
    are said to be "non-*sat*" (*asat*),
and they are nothing,
    either here in this world or hereafter.

18

The Final Teachings and Conclusion

Arjuna said:

(1) I want to know the truth in detail

concerning renunciation (*samnyāsa*)

and abandonment (*tyāga*).

Renunciation and Abandonment of Worldly Goods

The Blessed Lord said:

(2) Those who know declare

the renunciation of acts

resulting from desire to be true renunciation.

The giving up of all fruits of action

the wise call true abandonment.

(1–2) Renunciation, abandonment and nonattached action. The *Bhagavad Gītā* has already made it clear that true renunciation is not renunciation of action but renunciation of all attachment to the fruits of action. At the time the Gītā was written, those men and women who were intent on the attainment of liberation from bondage to continuing rebirth were usually expected not only to renounce the goods and goals of the worldly life; they were also generally expected to abandon all worldly activities. The Gītā explains both renunciation and abandonment of worldly goods and activities in terms of nonattached action.

(3) Some men of wisdom say
> that all actions should be abandoned as evil;

others say that acts of worship,
> of charity (*dāna*, "giving"),

> and of austerity must not be given up

> but should be performed.

Abandonment of Worldly Actions

(4) Hear now My answer to the question
> of the abandonment of actions,

for this abandonment is declared to be threefold.

Perform Acts of Worship, Charity, and Austerity

(5) Acts of worship, of charity and of austerity
> must not be given up but should be performed,

for worship, charity, and austerity
> are purifiers of the wise.

Perform These Acts Without Attachment

(6) But these actions must also be performed
> with abandonment of all attachment
>> to their fruits—

this is My distinct, final conclusion.

Three Kinds of Renunciation: Tamasic Renunciation

(7) For renunciation of action
    that is ordained is not right;
renouncing such actions because of delusion
    is said to be of *tamas*.

Rejasic Renunciation

(8) That which a man gives up
    merely because it is unpleasant
    or from fear of bodily harm,
such a man's renunciation
    is of the nature of *rajas*,
    and he will get no fruit at all
    from this kind of renunciation.

Sattvic Renunciation

(9) When necessary action is done
    simply because it ought to be done,
    having given up both attachment
    and the fruits of action,
that renunciation is understood
    to be of *sattva*.

True Abandonment

(10) He does not reject unpleasant action,

    and neither does he cling to pleasant action—

the man of true abandonment, wise,

    saturated throughout with *sattva*,

    all his doubts extinguished.

Complete Inaction Not Possible

(11) No one maintaining a body

    can give up actions completely,

but he who gives up the fruit of action

    is declared to be a man of true abandonment.

Three Kinds of Fruits of Action

(12) Undersirable, desirable, and mixed—

    of three kinds is the fruit

    of action after death

    for those who are not men of true abandonment,

but not for those

    who are men of true renunciation.

(12) The fruits of action after death. Here the *Bhagavad Gītā* presents a threefold analysis of human action which is not based on the nature and effects of the three *gunas*. The point is simply that the man of true renunciation and abandonment is not concerned for the fruits of his actions of whatever kind and whether in this life or after death. Note too that renunciation and abandonment have both been identified with nonattachment to the fruits of action.

The Five Elements of All Action

(13) Analytical philosophy (*sāmkhya*) declares

    the following five elements to be necessary

    for the effective performance of all actions—

learn now from Me.

(14) Their foundation in *prakriti*

    and also the doer himself,

    the various kinds of instruments of action,

    the various distinct kinds of movements,

and, as the fifth,

    the divinely ordained dispensation

    of things (*daivam*).

(15) Whatever action men engage in

    with body, speech, or mind,

    and whether lawful or unlawful,

these are the five elements of that action.

(13–15) Analysis of the nature of an action. The point of this summary analysis of the nature of all action is that every constituent of it is composed of the *gunas* of *prakriti* and has nothing to do with the supreme Self. Even "*daivam*," literally "of the deities," which I translate as the "divinely ordained dispensation of things," consists of the order and lawfulness of the *gunas* and their modifications throughout the universe.

The Ego-self Not the Sole Doer of Actions

(16) This being the case,
>whoever sees himself alone
>
>as the doer in this world,

he is a man of perverted *buddhi*,
>he is a fool,
>
>and he does not see truly.

(17) But whoever is not egotistical,
>whose *buddhi* is not contaminated,

even if he kills those people here before us,
>he does not kill,
>
>and he is not bound.

Knowledge and Action

(18) Knowledge, the object of knowledge,
>and the knower
>
>make up the threefold impulse to action;

instrument, act, and doer
>form the threefold integration (*samgraha*)
>
>of action itself.

Knowledge, Action, and Doer of Action

(19) There are three kinds of knowledge,

> three kinds of action,

> and three kinds of doers of action,

in correlation with the differences

> in the three *gunas*.

(18–19) Three kinds of knowledge, action, and doer of action. We learned earlier that according to the *Bhagavad Gītā* "all action without exception culminates in knowledge" (IV.33); here we are told that knowledge is involved as causal when action occurs, and then the Gītā proceeds in the *shlokas* that follow with an analysis of knowledge, action, and the doer in the now-familiar threefold distinction according to the nature and effects of each of the *gunas*.

Sattvic Knowledge

(20) Know that that knowledge is of *sattva*

> whereby men apprehend the one eternal Being

> within all creatures,

the undivided in the midst of diversity.

Rajasic Knowledge

(21) But know that that knowledge is of *rajas*

which sees in all creatures

> only differences of various kinds.

Tamasic Knowledge

(22) And that knowledge is declared to be of *tamas*
which is without reason,
> is not concerned with the essential
> truth (*tattva*),
> and is of no consequence,
> obsessed by one goal
> as though it were everything.

Sattvic Action

(23) Action derived from *sattva*
> is said to be that which is righteous
> and free from attachment,

done without either desire or aversion
> and without seeking any fruits from it.

Rajasic Action

(24) Action derived from *rajas*
> is done by a selfish person
> seeking the satisfaction of his desires

or, alternatively, with great and exhausting labor.

Tamasic Action

(25) Action derived from *tamas*
>is undertaken out of delusion
>and without regard for the consequences
>such as possible loss or injury

and without regard
>even for the doer's own ability.

The Sattvic Doer

(26) Free of attachment,
>without concern for himself,
>firm of purpose and energetic,
>unmoved by either success or failure—

this kind of doer is called a man of *sattva*.

The Rajasic Doer

(27) Passionate and seeking the fruits of his actions,
>avaricious, violent, and impure,
>alternating between the heights of pleasure
>and the depths of misery—

this kind of doer is well known
>to be a man of *rajas*.

The Tamasic Doer

(28) Undisciplined, vulgar, stubborn,

    deceitful, dishonest, lazy,

    emotional, and procrastinating—

such a doer is said to be a man of *tamas*.

Three Kinds of Buddhi and Firmness of Purpose

(29) Now hear completely explained

    the threefold distinction of both *buddhi*

    and firmness of purpose (*dhṛtiḥ*),

in their various forms

    in correlation with the *gunas*.

The Sattvic Buddhi

(30) The *buddhi* which understands action and nonaction,

    what is to be done and what is not to be done,

    danger and freedom from danger,

    bondage and liberation,

that is the *buddhi* of *sattva*.

The Rajasic Buddhi

(31) That *buddhi* is of *rajas*

    by means of which righteousness

    and unrighteousness,

what is to be done

    and what is not to be done

    are wrongly understood.

The Tamasic Buddhi

(32) That *buddhi* is of *tamas*

which, covered by darkness,

believes righteousness to be unrighteousness

and everything contrary to fact.

Sattvic Firmness of Purpose

(33) The firmness of purpose with which,

in unfaltering discipline,

one controls the actions of the *manas*,

the vital forces (*prānāh*), and the senses,

that firmness of purpose is of *sattva*.

Rajasic Firmness of Purpose

(34) But when it holds stubbornly

to duty, desire, and material goods,

with attachment and desire

for the fruits of action,

that firmness of purpose is of *rajas*.

Tamasic Firmness of Purpose

(35) That firmness of purpose by means of which

the fool does not give up sleep,

fear, grief, gloom, and egotism—

that firmness of purpose is of *tamas*.

(20–35) **Proper and improper character and conduct.** These correlations of human characteristics with the three *gunas* have served the purpose of telling Arjuna and the reader what kinds of character and conduct are and are not proper and effective for the attainment of the highest human good. The correlations which now follow inform him of the kinds of happiness resulting from each kind of character and conduct.

Three Kinds of Happiness

(36) But now hear from Me

>the three kinds of happiness.

That in which one delights

>as the result of long, disciplined

>practice of yoga

>and in which one comes to the end of suffering,

Sattvic Happiness

(37) which at first is like poison

>but at the end is like nectar,

>born of a peaceful spirit (*ātma*) and *buddhi*,

that happiness is proclaimed to be of *sattva*.

Rajasic Happiness

(38) That happiness which comes

>from the conjunction of the senses

>with their objects,

>which at first is like nectar

>but in the end is like poison,

one knows that happiness to be of *rajas*.

Tamasic Happiness

(39) And that happiness which

    both in the beginning

    and in the end is self-deluded,

  arising from sleep, laziness, and carelessness,

that happiness is said to be of *tamas*.

The Gunas Are All-inclusive

(40) There is nothing on earth

    or even among the deities in heaven,

  no being whatever that could ever be free

    of these three *gunas*

      originating from *prakriti*.

(40) "Freedom" from the gunas by transcendence of them. In Chapter Two we were told that we "must be free of the *gunas*, free of the dualities (*dvandvas*)" (.45) if we are to attain the supreme good; yet here the Gītā tells us that nothing whatever in the entire universe (including the deities in heaven) can ever be free of the three *gunas*. The point of the present statement concerning the omnipresence of the *gunas* is simply to emphasize the fact that according to the Gītā all of phenomenal existence is composed of the *gunas* of *prakriti*. Human beings *can* be free of them, however, because the practiced yogi can transcend them by means of that evenness of mind which we have learned is the essence of yoga. The *shlokas* which follow now specify the effects of the nature of the *gunas* on human society itself, in the form of the traditional four classes of the Indian people.

The Gunas and the Four Classes

(41)   The actions of Brahmins,

     Kshatriyas, Vaishyas, and *Shūdras*

     are distinguished according to the *gunas*

that arise from their own nature.

(41) The four classes and the gunas. As we have seen earlier, the Brahmins (*Brāhmanas*) are the priests and teachers of the traditional Indian society; *Kshatriyas* are the rulers, warriors, and administrators; *Vaishyas* are merchants and farmers; and the *Shūdras* are servants and laborers. The Gītā now specifies their duties, activities, and personal characteristics according to the *gunas* which are said to predominate in the persons of each of the classes.

Characteristics of Brahmins

(42)   Calmness, self-control, austerity,

     purity, patience and righteousness,

     wisdom, knowledge, and faith—

these qualities characterize the actions

     to which Brahmins are born.

. . . Kshatriyas

(43)   Heroism, dignity, firmness, skill,

     courage in battle,

     generosity, and a lordly nature

characterize the actions

     to which those of the *Kshatriya* class are born.

... Vaishyas and Shūdras

(44) Agriculture, the tending of cattle, and commerce
 constitute the work
 to which those of the third class are born.
In like manner, work consisting of service to others
 is innate to people of the *Shūdra* class.

Delighting in One's Own Work

(45) Delighting in his own individual work,
 a man attains perfection.
Hear now how a man attains perfection
 delighting in his own work.

Doing One's Own Work as an Act of Worship

(46) Him from Whom comes the existence
 of all creatures,
 by whom all this world is pervaded—
worshipping Him by means of one's own work,
 a man attains perfection.

(45–46) Delight in one's own individual work and human perfection. It is clear that "one's own individual work" is here first presented as the work of one's class. But it is equally clear that one's actual work is uniquely one's own, for the phrase that I have translated as "one's own individual work" is "*sva sva karma*," literally "own, own work," which emphasizes its uniqueness to the individual. Further, we know that everything we do, including our own work, is done by our own individual nature, *svabhāva*, composed of the three *gunas*. It is clear too that the individual should take real and active delight in doing his work and doing it skillfully and well, so that it may be offered to the Lord as sacrifice or worship. "Delighting in his own individual work," then, and offering it to the Lord in this manner, a human being is said to be able to attain perfection. The *shloka* which now follows reemphasizes the importance of doing one's own individual duty, in almost the same words the Gītā employed for this purpose in Chapter Three (.35).

One's Own Duty

(47) One's own duty,

> even if it is imperfectly done,
>
> is better than the duty of another
>
> well performed.

Performing actions required by his own nature,

> a man gets no evil.

Never Give Up Your Own Work

(48) One should not give up his own natural work

> even it it is imperfect,

since all enterprises are clouded by flaws

> like fire by smoke.

Perfection of Nonattached Action

(49) His *buddhi* without attachment

    to anything at all

    his self conquered,

    free from cravings,

he comes by means of true renunciation

    to the highest perfection

    of nonattached action (*naiṣkarmya*, "actionlessness").

(49) One's own work, one's own duty, and karma yoga. This *shloka* summarizes the nature of karma yoga and puts the teachings concerning one's own individual work and duty in the context of that discipline, as did the earlier counsel to do one's work as worship.

Attainment of Brahman

(50) Now hear from Me, very briefly,

    how the man who has attained to perfection

    also quickly attains to *brahman*,

which is the highest effect of knowledge.

(50) Attainment of the highest good by means of knowledge (*jñāna*, "unitive knowledge"). Here the *Bhagavad Gītā* makes it clear that even perfection in one's own work and in the discipline of nonattached action is not, of itself, the attainment of the supreme good but a primary means to that attainment. But such perfection does therefore result in that unitive knowledge of *brahman* which is the final means to the attainment of the highest good.

How Such a Man Acts

(51) With purified *buddhi*,

    disciplined and firmly controlling himself,

giving up the objects of the senses,

    mere words, and the rest of the distractions,

    discarding all desires and aversions,

(52) resorting to solitude, eating lightly,

    controlling his speech, his body, and his mind,

being constantly devoted to the yoga

    of meditation-contemplation,

    resorting to dispassion,

(53) liberated from all egotism,

    violence, pride, desire, anger,

    and possessiveness,

    remaining calm and unselfish,

he is worthy of becoming *brahman*.

(52–53) Dhyāna yoga as means to the attainment of brahman. Here the Gītā counsels the use of *dhyāna* yoga, the discipline of meditation-contemplation outlined in Chapter Six, to effect the final unitive experience of *brahma-nirvāna*. But in the *shlokas* immediately following this recommendation of *dhyāna* yoga, the Gītā presents its final teaching concerning the insuperable effectiveness of *bhakti* yoga, the discipline of selfless devotion to deity, which, according to the *Bhagavad Gītā*, constitutes the highest achievement of yoga attainable by human beings.

Devotion to Krishna as Lord (Īśvara)

(54) Having become *brahman*,

    his self tranquil,

    he then neither grieves nor craves;

the same to all creatures,

    he comes to supreme devotion

    (*para bhakti*) to Me.

(55) By means of his devotion to Me,

    he comes to know Me—

    what My power is

    and Who I really am.

Then, knowing Me in the fullness of truth,

    he immediately enters into Me.

Devotion and Nonattached Action

(56) Even though he always performs all actions,

he reaches the eternal deathless state by My grace.

Establishing the Self in Krishna

(57) Willingly giving up all your actions to Me,

    devoted to Me

    and resorting to the discipline of the *buddhi*,

keep your consciousness fixed always in Me.

(58) For as long as your consciousness is fixed in Me,
> you shall overcome all difficulties by My grace.
> But if because of egotism
>> you pay no attention to Me,
>> you will perish.

(59) For if you cling to egotism
> and think, 'I will not fight',
> this resolution of yours is in vain—
> your own nature will compel you.

One's Nature Demands Its Own Action

(60) Bound by your own natural action,
> whatever you try to avoid doing
> because of delusion,
> that you will nevertheless do
>> even against your will.

The Lord Dwells in the Hearts of All

(61) The Lord of all creatures
> dwells in the heart of all creatures;
> and by means of His power
>> He moves the entire universe
>> as ordained in the divine order
>> of things (*daivam*).

The Final Teachings and Conclusion 235

(62) Therefore go with your entire being

    to Him only for refuge—

you will attain supreme peace

    and the undying state by His grace.

Now Act as You Think Best

(63) Thus have I explained to you that wisdom

    which is the most secret secret:

after studying this wisdom most thoroughly,

    you should then act as you think best.

(63) Listen to the wisdom of the Lord but act as you think best! This last *shloka* must certainly be one of the most remarkable passages to be found in scripture anywhere, for though this "most secret secret"—and indeed the Gītā's teachings throughout—have been given by the Divine Teacher, the Lord himself, the *Bhagavad Gītā* now tells us to act as we think best after carefully considering these teachings; it does not tell us to do as we are told, even by the Lord.

Devotion to Deity Is Best

(64) Again, hear the highest secret of all,

    My supreme Word.

Since you are greatly beloved by Me,

    I shall therefore declare your highest welfare.

(65) Be of My mind, devoted to Me;
> worship Me and revere Me,
> and you shall come to Me only—

this I promise you in truth,
> because you are dear to Me.

(66) Giving up all other duties (*dharmān*),
> come to Me as your one refuge:

do not grieve—
> I will save you from all evils.

This Teaching for the Devout Only

(67) This must not be told
> to one not given to austerity

and never to one without devotion
> or to anyone who is not obedient—
> nor to anyone who speaks against Me.

Those Who Teach This Doctrine

(68) Whoever shall teach this
> supreme secret to My devotees,
> showing the highest devotion to Me,

without doubt he will come to Me only.

(69) And there is no one among men
> who does anything that is dearer to Me,

nor shall there be anyone in this world
> dearer to Me than he is.

Study the Gītā with the Sacrifice of Knowledge

(70) Whoever shall study this,

    our colloquy on *dharma*,

I maintain that he should worship Me

    with knowledge.

(71) Full of faith

    and not complaining about it,

    whatever person even hears this teaching,

    he also shall be liberated,

and he will attain to the bright worlds

    of men of meritorious actions.

(71) "Liberation" from hearing this teaching. Note that "liberation" of those who merely hear this teaching even if they are devoted to the Lord, is not the ultimate good and goal but simply the reward of those who performed meritorious actions, a temporary residence in the "bright worlds" or heavens, before being reborn to continue seeking full and final liberation from all birth, death, and rebirth.

A Final Question to Arjuna

(72) Have you heard this

    with concentrated consciousness?

Have your great confusion

    and ignorance been done away with?

The Proper Answer to Krishna's Question

Arjuna said:

(73) The delusion has been destroyed—

> by Your grace

> I have attained knowledge.

All my doubts removed

> I now stand firm:

> I will do as You have taught.

(73) The conclusion of the teachings of the Bhagavad Gītā. This *shloka* marks the conclusion of the teachings of the Gītā. The five final *shlokas* which follow constitute a kind of epilogue in which Sanjaya, the narrator of the dialogue, refers to Krishna as "the Lord of yoga" and emphasizes the value of the teachings presented in the dialogue.

Sanjaya said:

(74) In this manner have I heard

> this wonderful and moving dialogue

of Krishna and the highly honored Arjuna.

(75) I have heard this highest secret by the grace

> of (the legendary sage) Vyāsa—

this yoga from Krishna, the Lord of yoga,

> He Himself declaring it in person.

The Final Teachings and Conclusion

(76) O King (Dhritarashtra), when I remember

again and again

this wonderful and blessed dialogue

of Krishna and Arjuna,

I tremble with joy

at each instant of it.

(77) And as I remember again and again

Krishna's most wonderful Form,

I am greatly amazed, O King,

and I am again and again thrilled with joy.

(78) Wherever Krishna, Lord of disciples, is

and wherever Arjuna is, that great bowman,

I know that there good fortune, victory, prosperity,

and statesmanship are firmly established.

Index

Roman numerals refer to chapters of the *Bhagavad Gītā*; arabic numerals refer to specific *shlokas* (stanzas) of the text. Key passage numbers are italicized.

abhyāsa. See Practice, yogic
Action (*karma*). II.*47–50*, .51, .64; III.1, .9, .14–.17, .24, .26 f., .28, .30 f.; IV.7–.9, *.13–.23*, .32 f., .37, .41 f.; V.1–.3, .7, .12–.14; VI.1–.4, .17, .40 f., .45 f.; VII.3., .28 f.; VIII.1, .3; IX.9, .27 f., .30 f.; XI.*55*; XII.5 f., .10; XIII.20, *.29*, .31; XIV.7, .9, .12–.16, .19, .21 f., .23, .25; XV.2, .4, *.20*; XVI.7, .22–.24; XVII. 4, .23–.26, .28; XVIII.2–.3, .5–.15, .18, .23–.28, .30–.32, .33, .41–.44, *.45–.49*, .56 f., .60, *.63*, .69, .71, .73
Action, fruits of (*karmaphala*). II.43, .17, .49, .51; III.7, .9, .31; IV.14, .20; V.3, .6, .12, .14, *.20*; VIII.28; IX.28; XII.11 f.; XIV.*16*; XVII.11 f., .17, .21, .25; XVIII.2, .6, .8 f., .11 f., .23, .27, .34
Action, one's own individual (*svakarma, svasvakarma*). XVIII. *45–49*
akshara. See Immutable, the
amritatva. See Deathlessness
asakti. See Nonattachment
asanga. See Nonattachment
ātman. See Self, phenomenal and Self, the supreme

Attraction-and-aversion (*rāgadveśa*). II.64; III.34; VII.27; XIII.6; XVIII.23, .51
Austerity (*tapas*). IV.10, .28; V.30; VI.46; VII.9; VIII.11, .28; IX.27; XVI.1; XVII.*5–.6*, .14–.19, .24 f., .27 f.; XVIII. 3, *.5*, .67
Avatar (*avatāra*). IV.*7 f.*
avatāra. See Avatar

bandha. See Bondage
bhakti. See Devotion, selfless
bhūtā. See Creatures
Body (*deha, sharīra*). II.13, .18, .22; IV.9; XIII.*1–.6*, .26, .31 f., .34; XIV.20; XV.2, .8; XVII.6, .14; XVIII.11, .15, .52
Bondage (*bandha, karmabandha*). II.39; III.9; IV.14: V.3, .12; IX.28; XIV.*5–.8*; XVI.5; XVIII.17, .30, .60
brahman. See Reality, absolute
buddhi. See Intelligence-will

citta. See Mind-stuff
Class, classes (*varna, varnāh*). IV.13; IX.32 f.; XVIII.*41–44*
Consciousness, concentration of

Consciousness (*continued*)
(*samādhi*). II.44, .53, .66; VI.7, .18; VIII.12; XVII.11; XVIII.72
Consciousness, phenomenal (*cetanā, ceta, citta,* etc.). II.7, .44, .65; III.30; IV.21, .23; V.16, .19, .26; VI.10, .14, .18–.20, .23; VII.30; VIII.7 f., .10, .14; X.9; XII.5., .7, .9, .19; XIII.6; XV.11; XVII.19; XVIII.57 f., .72
Creatures (*bhūtā*). II.28, .69; III.10, .18, .24, *.33*; IV.35; V.7, .15, .18 f., *.25*, .29; VI.29, .31; VII.6, .9 f., .26 f., .30; VIII.1, .4, *.18–.19*, .22; IX.*4–8*; X.5 f., .20; XI.9; XII.4; XIII.16, .26, .34; XIV.8; XV.4, .16; XVI.2, .6; XVIII.20 f., .46, .54, .61
Cycles, cosmic (*kalpa, yuga*). IV.8; VIII.*17–.19*; IX.7; XIV.2

daivam. See Order of the universe, the divine
Deathlessness (*amritatva*). II.15; XIII.*12*; XIV.20; XVIII.56
deha. See Body
dehī. See Embodied One, the
Delusion (*moha,* etc.). II.13, .19, .44, .52, 62 f., .70, .72; III.24, .27, .32, .40; IV. 16, .55; V.15, *.20*; VI.37; VII.13, .15, .25, *.27*; VIII.27; IX.12; X.3 f.; XI.1; XIV.8, .13, .15, .17, .22; XV.5, .10 f., .19; XVI.10, .16, .20; XVII.19; XVIII.7, .25, .39, .60, .73
Demonic natures (*āsurāh*). VII.15; XVI.4, *.6–.8*
Desire (*rāga*). II.43, *.55–.57*, .62, .64, 70 f; III.30, .34, *.37–.41*, .43; IV.10, .12, .19, .21; V.3, .12, .23, .26, .28; VI.10, .18, .24; VII.11, .20, .22, .27; VIII.11; IX.21; XII.17; XIII.6; XIV.7 ., 12, .17, .22; XV.5; XVI.2, *.8*, .10–.16, .18, .21, .23; XVII.5, .11; XVIII.2, .24, .27, .34, .49, .51, .53
Devotion, selfess (*bhakti*). IV.3, *.9–.11*, .33, .35; V.17; VI..*30 f.*, .47; VII.1, .14, .17, .23; VIII.10, .13 f., *.22*; IX.*22–.27*, *.29–.31*; X.8; XI.53–55; XII.1, .6, .17, .19 f; XIII.10, .18, .25; XIV.*26*; XV.*19*; XVIII.54–.58, .62, .65–.68

dharma. See Duty, rightousness. See also Duty, one's own individual
dhriti. See Purpose, firmness of
dhyāna. See Meditation-contemplation
Discipline, disciplined (*yoga, yukta*). II.39, *.48–.50*, .61; III.3, .26; IV.1–3, .18, .27, .38, .41 f.; V.1 f., *.4–.8*, .11 f., *.21–.24*; VI.*1–.4*, .8, .10, .12, *.14–20*, .23, .25, *.27–.29*, *.31–.33*, .37, .41 f., .44 f., .47; VII.1, .17 f., .22, .30; VIII.2, *.8*, .10, .12, .14, .23, .25, .27 f.; IX.14, .28, .34; X.7, .10; XII.1–.2, .6, .9, .11, .14; XIII.10, .24; XV.11; XVII.17; XVIII.28, .33, .36, .51, .57
Discipline of nonattached action, the (*karma yoga*). II.14, .38, *.40*, .47 f., *.50*, .57; III.3 f., .7, *.18–.19*, *.25*; IV.12, .15, *.20*, .38, .41; V.1 f., .4 f., *.8–.13*; VI.*1–.4*, .33, .36, .46; IX.9, .28; XI.*55*; XII.9 f.; XIII.*24*; XIV.*22–.25*
Dispassion (*vairāga*). VI.*35*; VIII.11; XIII.8; XVIII.52
Dualities (*dvandvā*). II.14–15, .38, .45, .57, .64; III.34, .37; IV.22; V.3, .20, .23, .26; VI.7, .32; VII.11, *.27–28*; XIII.6, .9, .20 f.;

XIV.24 f.; XV.5; XVI.12, .18; XVIII.10, .28 f., .30–32, .51, .54
Duty, one's own individual (*svadharma*). II.31; III.*35*; XVIII.47
Duty, righteousness (*dharma*). I.*1*; II.7, .31; IV.7 f., VI.40; VII.11; IX.3; XIV.27; XVI.1; XVIII.23, .31 f., 34, .66
dvandva. See Dualities

Elements of matter, the. VII.*4*
Embodied One, the (*dehī*). II.13, .18, .22, .30; III.40 f.; V.13; XIV.7
Evil and wickedness (*pāpam*). II.38, .50; III.13, .16, .21, .30, .36; V.10, .15, .17, .25; VI.9, .40; VII.15, .28; IX.1, .*30*; X.3; XIII.*8*, .21; XIV.6; XV.5; XVI.19; XVIII.3, .47, .66

Faith (*shraddhā*). III.31; IV.39 f.; V.25; VI.37, .47; VII.21 f.; IX.3, .23; XII.2, .20; XVII.*1–.4*, .13, .17, .28; XVIII.42, .71
Food and diet. IV.30; VI.*16–17*; XVII.7–.10, .13

Giving, charity (*dāna*). VIII.29; IX.27; XVII.7, .20, .24 f.; XVIII.3, .5
gunāh. See Matter, constituents of

Happiness. II.66; IV.40; V.*21*, .*23* f., .40; VI.*21*–.*23*, .27 f.; X.9: XII.18; XIV.6, .9, .27; XVI.23; XVII.8; XVIII.*36–.39*
"Heart" as center of consciousness. IV.42; VIII.12; X.20; XIII.17; XV.15; XVIII.61

Ignorance (*avidyā*). III.26, .29, .32; IV.40, .42; V.15 f.; VII.15, .24; IX.12; X.11; XIII.11; XIV.8, .16; XVI.4; XVIII.72
Immanence of the one transcendental Reality (*brahman*, Krishna, etc.) VIII.22; IX.4; XIII.15 f, .*17*; XVIII.46, .*61*
Immutable, the (*akshara*). III.15; VIII.3
Imperishable, the (*avyaya*). II.17; VII.25; VIII.11; XII.3
Independence of the yogi. III.*18*; IV.20, .22; XII.14, .19
Individual human being, constituents of the. III.42 f.; XIII.1, .*5 f.*
"Integration of the world (*lokasamgraha*)." III.20, .30
Intellect-will (*buddhi*). II.39 f., .*41*, .49–.54, .62, 65 f.; III.1 f., .26, .40, .*42*; V.11, 17, .20, .28; VI.9, 21, .25, .43; VII.4, .10; VIII.7; X.10; XII.4, .8, .14; XIII.*5*; XVIII.16, .*29–32*, .37, .49, .51, .57
īswara. See Lord, the

jīva. See Person, the living
jīvātman. See Person, the living
jñāna. See Knowledge, unitive

kalpāh. See Cycles, cosmic
karma. See Action
karmaphala. See Action, fruits of
karma yoga. See Discipline of nonattached action, the
Knowledge, phenomenal (*vijñāna*).

Knowledge (*continued*)
II.19, .44, .46, .60, .69; III.3, .28, .41; IV.14 f., .16 f; V.5; VI.8, 23, .32; VII.2, .23; VIII.27; IX.*1 f.*; X.2 f.; XII.1; XIII.4, .29; XV.2; XVIII.29 f., .42., .*63*

Knowledge, unitive (*jñāna*). II.11, .16, .69; III.3, .29, .33; IV.16 f., .19, .23, .27, *.35–.39*, .41 f.; V.*15–.17*, .26; VI.8, .46; VII.2, *.15–.20*, *.29 f.*; VIII.11; IX.*1*, .11; X.7; XII.12, .19; XIII.1, .11f, *.17 f.*, .24 f.; XIV. 1 f., .6, .9, .11, .14, .17; XV.10, *.19 f.*; XVI.1; XVII.24; XVIII.*18–.22*, .42, .50–.55, .70, .73

Krishna as deity. II.61; III.*22–.24*; IV.1, .6, *.7 f.*, .11 f.; V.14 f., .29; VI.30 f.; VII.3, *.4–.7*, .12 f., *.18–.19*, .21f., *.24–.26*, .30: VIII.1, *.3–.5*, *.8 .21 f.*; IX.*3–.8*, .11, .15, *.18*, *.23–.24*, .29; X.*2–.3*, .6, .8, .20, .42; XI *passim*; XII.7; XIII.2, .27; XIV.3 f., .19, .27; XV.7, *.8–.10*, *.17–.19*; XVI.19; XVII.6; XVIII.6, *.61*, .66

Law, scriptural (śāstra). XVI.*24*; XVII.1; XVIII.15

Liberation (*moksha, mukti*). II.*45*; III.13, .30 f.; IV.15, .23, .32; V.3, .23, .28; VI.10, .14, .18, .28; VII.28 f.; IX.1, .28; X.3: XI.55; XII.13, .15, .18; XIII.9; XIV.6, .20; XV.5; XVI.5, .20; XVII.25; XVIII.26, .30, .53, .71

Life-force (*prāna*). IV.29; V.27; VIII.10, .12; X.9; XVIII.33

Life-force, control of (*prānāyāma*). IV.29; V.27; VIII. 10 f.

lokamaheshvara. See Lord, the
lokasamgraha. See "Integration of the world"

Lord, the (īśvara, lokameśvara). IV.6; V.29; IX.11, .24; X.3; XIII.22, *.27 f.*; XV.8; XVI.8; XVIII.46, .61

manas. See Mind, sense-mind

Matter, constituents of (*gunāh*). II.45; III.13; V.*21*, *.23 f.*, .33; IV.13; VII.12–14, .25; XIII.14. .19–.23, *.29*; XIV.*5–.20*, *.21.–.26*; XV.2, .10; XVIII..*7–.10*, .19, .40

Matter, undifferentiated (*prakriti*). III.27, .29, .33; IV.6; VII.4 f., .13; IX.7 f., .10; XIII.*19–23*, *.26*, .34; XIV.5; XV.7

māyā. See World, illusoriness of

Meditation-contemplation (*dhyāna*). V.27; VI.*10–.17*; VIII.9, .12; XII.12; XIII.24; XVIII.52

Mind, evenness of (*samatva*). II.15, .38. *,48*, .57; IV.22; V.18–20; VI.3, *.7–.9*, .22 f., 29, .32 f.,; XI.9, .29; X.5; XII.4., .13, .18 f.; XIII.9, .28; XIV.4, .13, .18 f., *.23–.26*; XVIII.10, .26, *.54*

Mind, sense-mind (*manas*). II.55 f., .60, .67; III.6 f., .40, .42; V.11, .13, .28; VI.12, .14, .24–.27, .34 f., 45; VII.4; VIII.7, .12; IX.34; XII.2, .8, .14; XIV.11; XV.7, .9; XVIII.*24–.25*

Nature, one's own individual (*svabhāva*). II.7; III.*33*; V.*14*, .19; VII.20; VIII.3; XVII.2 f.; XVIII.41, .47, .59

Philosophy, analytical (*sāmkhya*). II.39; III.3; V.*4 f.*; XVIII.13, .19

Index

Pleasure-pain (*sukha-duhkha*).
  II.15; V.22; VI.7, .32; XII.13;
  XIII.6; XIV.24; XV.5; XVIII.27
Practice (*abhyāsa*). VI.*35*, .44;
  VIII.8; IX.2; XVIII.36
prakriti. See Matter, undifferentiated
prāna. See Life-force
prānāyāma. See Life-force, control of
punarjanma. See Rebirth
Purification of the phenomenal self.
  IV.10, .19, .37 f.; V.7, *.11*, .27;
  VI.12, .45; VIII.10 f.; IX.2, .20;
  XVI.1; XVIII.5, .51
Purpose, firmness of (*dhriti*). II.37,
  .41, .44; VI.23; IX.14, .30;
  XII.14; XVI.2; XVIII.26, .59, .73
puruśa. See Spirit
purushottama. See Lord, the

rāga. See Desire
rāgadvesha See Attraction-and-aversion
rajas-guna (activity, energy).
  III.37, VI.27; VII.12; XIV.5, .7,
  .9 f., .12, .15–18; XVII.1, .4, .9,
  .12, .18, .21; XVIII.8, .21, .24,
  .27, .31, .34, .38
Reality, absolute (*brahman*). II.72;
  III.15; IV.24; V.6, .18, .19 f.,
  .21, .24; VII.29; VIII.3, .13, .17–
  .19; XIII.*12*–*.18*, .30; XIV.3 f.,
  .26 f; XVII.23; XVIII.50, .53 f.
Reality, phenomenal. II.*18*–*.30*;
  III.30; V.7, .20, .23 f., .29;
  VII.29; VIII.3, .9; X.20, XIII.11,
  .22, .24, .27, .31: XIV.7, .20;
  XV.5
Reality, phenomenal, as *māyā*.
  IV.6; VII.14 f., .25
Rebirth (*punarjanma*). II.*22*–*.27*,
  .43; IV.5, .9; V.17; VI.*37*–*.45*;
  VII.19; VIII.15 f., .21; IX.3;
  XII.7; XV.4, *.7*–*.11*; XVI.20
Renunciation (*sannyāsa*). II.47,
  .50; III.4 f., .8, *.17*, .30; IV.41;
  V.2 f.; VI.1 f., .4; IX.28; XII.12,
  .16 f.; XVIII.*1 f.*, .59, .73
Resignation (*tyāga*). II.48, *.51*, .71;
  IV.20 f.; V.10, .12 f., .28; VI.21,
  .24; XII.11; XIV.25; XVI.21;
  XVIII.*3*–.6, .9–.12, .51, .57
Resolution (*vavasaya*). II.37, *.41*,
  .44; VI.23; IX.14, .30; XII.14;
  XVI.2; XVIII.23, .59, .73

Sacrifice, worship (*yajna*). III.*9*–
  .14; IV.12, .23, *.24*–*.33*; V.10,
  .29; VI.1, .46; VII.21–.23, .30;
  VIII.2, .4, .28; IX.23, *.26 f.*, .34;
  X.8, .10; XII.1–.3, .6; XVI.1;
  XVII.7, .11–.13, .23–.25, .47 f.;
  XVIII.3, .5, *.46*, .65, *.70*
samādhi. See Consciousness, concentration of
samatva. See Mind, evenness of
sāmkhya. See Philosophy, analytical
samsāra. See Rebirth
sat-asat. See Reality, phenomenal
sannyāsa. See Renunciation
sattva-guna. II.45; VII.12; XIV.*5*–
  .6, .9–.11, .14, .16–.18; XVII.1,
  .4, .8, .11, .17, .20; XVIII.9 f.,
  .20, .23, .30, .33, .37
Self, phenomenal (*jīva*, *jīvātman*).
  XIII.*1*–*6*
Self, supreme (*paramātma*). II.*17*–
  .30, .29 f., .55; III.17, .28, .30,
  .42 f.; V.7, .21, .26; VI.18, .20,
  .25 f.; VIII.3, .8 f.; X.20; XII.3;
  XIII.11, *.22*, .24, *.27*–*.29*, *.31*–
  .33; XIV.14, .19 f.; XV.5, *.8*–*.11*,
  .17

Senses (*indriyāni*), sense-experience. II.8, .14 f., .58–.61, .64, .67 f.; III.6 f., .16, .34, .40 f.; IV.*26 f.*, .39; V.9, .9, .11, .21 f., .27 f.; VI.4, .8, .12 f., .21, 24 f.; VIII.12; XII.4; XIII.5, .8, .14; XIV.11; XV.2, .7, .9; XVIII.33, .38, .51
shabda. See Word, the divine
shāmya. See Mind, evenness of
shāntī. see Peace
shāstra. See Law, scriptural
shraddhā. See Faith
siddhi. See Perfection
Spirit (*puruśa*). VIII.4, .8, .10, .22; XIII.*19–.23*, *.26*; XV.*4*, *.16–.19*
sukha-duhkha. See Pleasure-pain
svabhāva. See Nature, one's own individual
svadharma. See Duty, one's own individual
svakarma. See Work, one's own individual

tamas-guna (dullness, heaviness). VII.12; XIV.*5*, *.8–.10*, .15–.18; XVII.1, .4, .10, .13, .19, .22; XVIII.7, .22, .25, .28, .32, .35, .39
tapas. See Austerity
tattva. See Truth
Transcendence, of the *gunas* (*gunātītya*). II.*45*; IV.22; VII.14; XIII.14, .31; XIV.*20–.2*
Truth, the essential (*tattva*). II.16; III.28; IV.9, .34; V.8; VII.3; IX.24; X.7; XI.54; XIII.11; XVI.2, .7 f.; XVIII.1, .22, .55, .65
tyāga. See Resignation

Unmanifest Reality (*avyakta*). II.25; VIII.*18*, *.20*; IX.4; XII.1, .3, .5; XIII.5

vairāgya. See Dispassion
Values (*puruśārthāh*). II.6 f., .43, .50; III.2; V.1, .15; VI.41; VII.16; X.1; XVII.15, .26; XVIII.22, .34, .64
varna. See Class, classes
vavasaya. See Resolution
vijnāna. See Knowledge, phenomenal

Word, the divine (*shabda*). VIII.11; XVII.15; XVIII.52, .64, .67
Work, one's own individual (*svakarma*). XVIII.*45–.48*, .60, .63
World, worlds (*loka, -āh*). II.17, .50; III.16, .22; IV.7, .12, .40; V.29; VI.40, .42; VII.2, *.5–.7*, .13, .25; VIII.16; IX.4, .10, .32; X.42; XIII.33; XIV.14, .18; XV.2 f., .7, .16 f.; XVI.6, .8; XVIII.16, .40, .46, .61, .69, .71

yajna. See Sacrifice
Yoga. II.39, *.48*, *.50*, .53; IV. 1–.3, .38, .41 f.; V.6, .21; VI.17, .20, *.23*, *.29*, .36 f., .41, .44; VII.20, .25; VIII.8, .12, .14, .27; IX.5; X.7; XII.12; XIII.*24 f.*
yuga. See Cycles, cosmic
yukta. See Disciplines, disciplined